THIS IS JESUS CHRIST

Also by Edward K. Watson

Is Jesus "God"? *A Witness to the World That Jesus is the Christ, the Eternal God* (in four volumes)

Ode to Jesus: *The Most Influential Person Who Ever Lived*

A Latter-day Saint Ode to Jesus: *The Most Influential Person Who Ever Lived*

Verifiable Evidence for the Book of Mormon: *Proof of Deliberate Design Within a Dictated Book*

The Holy Spirit: *The God Within Us*

The Iglesia Ni Cristo Under a Microscope: *Helping INC Members Keep More of Their Money, Survive Shunning, and Discover the Truth About Their Church and God*

Bliss: *A Guide for Women on Attracting and Keeping a Man*

Contentment: *A Guide for Couples on Maintaining a Great Companionship* (forthcoming, 2023)

The Adopted Children of God: *The Incomprehensible Fate of Christ's True Followers* (forthcoming, 2023)

10 Natural Rights: *Understanding Your Most Important Rights* (forthcoming, 2024)

How to Survive a Civilizational Collapse: *Baseline Survival Strategies* (forthcoming, 2024)

See www.edwardkwatson.com for more information.

THIS IS JESUS CHRIST

An <u>Interactive</u> Aid to Understanding the Holy Bible's Core Message

Edward K. Watson

Brainy-Press

Copyright © 2022 by Edward K. Watson.

All rights reserved. No part of this publication may be reproduced, stored in a retrieval system, or transmitted, in any form or by any means, electronic, mechanical, photocopying, recording, or otherwise, without the prior written permission of the author.

ISBN: 978-1-7779119-8-0

Cover design and all illustrations copyright © 2022, Edward K. Watson. Other photos and designs from Adobe Stock and Freekpik. Author photo copyright © 2022, Jeneffer M. Watson. All rights reserved.

Distributed by IngramSpark.

www.edwardkwatson.com

IMPORTANT!

1. All biblical quotations within THIS IS JESUS CHRIST are paraphrased text and came from this author's four-volume IS JESUS "GOD"? (Brainy Press).

   IS JESUS "GOD"? is a comprehensive examination of fifty-five (55) specific doctrines about Jesus that, when put together, shows the New Testament has a core message, a single soteriological cosmology centered on Jesus Christ. The work proves that the New Testament is a *frameless, unharmonized, correlative anthology* — an astonishing accomplishment without parallel in literature. This is the only empirical evidence that gives a very high probability that something supernatural was involved in the New Testament's creation.

2. This book uses "Jesus," "Christ," "Jesus Christ," "the Son of God," and "the Son" interchangeably.

The Holy Bible's Core Message or "Gospel"

God's only Son, JESUS CHRIST, the Creator of the universe who is "God" by nature – obeyed his Father's will and became human flesh. He then suffered and died to annul the Fall – when Adam and Eve transgressed and inflicted sin, death, moral weakness, and trials on humanity.

He rose from the dead to destroy death itself and make all humans immortal physical beings. He will then judge all humankind at the Last Day according to our works.

He conjoined the divine and human natures so that his grace allows some humans to be "adopted" by God, share ultimate glory, and participate in God's very nature, mutual indwelling, and oneness.

All who come unto JESUS CHRIST, repent of their sins, get baptized in his name, strive to live his teachings whereby the Holy Spirit within them continually refines and purifies them, and endure to the end will be rewarded with eternal bliss in his kingdom.

Table of Contents

Introduction 1

Part 1: Jesus Christ and His Importance .. 27

Jesus Made Your Life Better 29

You Have Natural Rights Thanks to Jesus Christ's Moral Teachings 29

The Modern STEM World is a Product of Jesus Christ's Moral Teachings 35

We Can Lose It All If We Do Not Resist .. 37

Is Jesus Still Relevant Today? 41

What Jesus Said About Himself 44

Part 2: Understanding Jesus Christ 49

Chapter 1: Jesus is "God" 53

1.1 Jesus Already Existed Before Becoming Human 53

1.2 Jesus Possessed the "God" Nature Before Becoming Human 58

1.3 Jesus Possessed "Glory" Before Creation 62

1.4 Jesus Causes the Forces of the Universe to Hold Together 65

1.5 Jesus Was Called "God" 70

1.6 Jesus Had the "God" Nature Within His Physical Body 77
1.7 Jesus Had Mutual Indwelling and "Oneness" With the Father 79
1.8 Jesus Gave Up His Glory to Become Human 84

Chapter 2: Jesus is the "Son of God" 87

2.1 Product of a Miraculous Pregnancy ... 87
2.2 Unique Relationship with God Before Becoming Human 91

Chapter 3: Jesus is Human 97

3.1 God (Jesus Christ) Became Human 97
3.2 The Son of God Became Human (*Homo sapiens sapiens*) 101
3.3 As a Human, Jesus Reconciles Us to God 105
3.4 Jesus Triumphed as a Human 108
3.5 Jesus Can Never Experience Death Again 110
3.6 Jesus Lives Forever with a Physical Body 112
3.7 Jesus Made a Single Sacrifice for All Time for All Humans 116

Chapter 4: Jesus is the Creator 121

    4.1 Jesus Created the Universe................ 122

    4.2 God the Father Created the Universe Through Jesus... 126

Chapter 5: Jesus Upgrades Earth 129

    5.1 The Earth Will Be Upgraded 129

Chapter 6: Jesus is the Savior 135

    6.1 Jesus Paid the Ransom for Humanity's Sins 135

    6.2 Jesus Suffered and Died as Our Sacrifice... 139

    6.3 Jesus Died for Humanity 144

    6.4 Jesus Christ's Sacrifice/Blood Reconciles Us to God 150

    6.5 Jesus Christ's Blood Forgives Sins.... 158

    6.6 Jesus Annuls Sin.................................. 162

    6.7 Jesus Christ's Grace Saves Us 165

    6.8 Jesus Condemned Sin Through His Flesh 167

    6.9 Jesus Saves Us From Our Sins........... 170

    6.10 Jesus Takes Away Our Sins............. 174

    6.11 Those Who Believe in Jesus Get Their Sins Forgiven 177

6.12 Consuming Christ's "Flesh" and "Blood" Saves Us 180

6.13 Jesus Reconciles Man to God 187

6.14 Jesus Intercedes/Mediates on Behalf of Man to God 190

Chapter 7: Jesus Conquered Death 195

7.1 Jesus Rose From the Dead 196

7.2 His Resurrection Saves Us From Death and Resurrects Us 203

7.3 Jesus Annulled the Devil and Controls Death and Access to the Afterlife 209

7.4 The Resurrected Jesus is Lord of Both the Living and the Dead 212

7.5 Jesus Destroys Death and Hades (the Afterlife) 215

Chapter 8: Jesus is the Only Way 217

8.1 No One Can be Saved or Approach God Without Going Through Jesus ... 217

Chapter 9: Jesus Shall Return 221

9.1 Jesus Shall Return to Earth 222

Chapter 10: Jesus Judges All 229

10.1 Jesus Judges Humanity 229

Conclusion **237**
Scripture Reference Guide **239**
Index **245**

Introduction

This book helps you understand Jesus Christ and why it is important to know him. But this work does not tell you what to believe; it only identifies what the Holy Bible says and lets you come to your own conclusions.

Your brain is a very powerful computer, and you possess the ability to make up your mind about what the biblical text is saying. Furthermore, as a human, you have the absolute right to believe whatever you want, and this book encourages you to write those beliefs down to solidify them and modify them as you grow and change. You do not need me or anyone else to tell you what to believe. Neither I nor anyone else has the moral right to say that you must interpret a passage in a certain way to be saved. Those who make such a dogmatic claim attempt to usurp God's judgment authority over you. They will be held accountable for their uncharitable nature when they stand before Christ on Judgment Day.

This book assumes what the Holy Bible says about Jesus is true and inspired by God. It asks questions—leading, to be sure—but with the intent to have you think and ponder about somber topics that can drastically change the trajectory of your life now and in the next realm.

A word of caution: While you have the right to believe whatever you want, be honest with yourself and apply that same honesty to how you interpret or understand the biblical text. This means if the text says "X," do not interpret it to mean "-X" or the opposite of what its face value is saying.

For example:

John 1:1-3,10,14 In the beginning was the Word; the Word existed with God; and the Word was God. 2 He existed with God in the beginning. 3 He created the universe. Nothing exists that he did not create. . . 10 He went and lived on Earth. And even though he created it, the world's inhabitants did not know who he was . . . 14 The Word became flesh and lived among us. We have seen his glory—the glory of the only Son of the Father, full of grace and truth.

This biblical passage says, "the Word was God." This same "Word" created the universe and Earth. He then lived in this world by becoming human and was known as "the only Son of the Father."

To be intellectually honest, you can interpret the passage however you want, *except the opposite* of what it says. Thus, you should not interpret the passage to mean the Word was not God, or he did not create the universe and Earth, or he did not become human, or he was not known as only Son of the Father.

A rule I follow is to use interpretations closest to the text's face value or what it is expressly saying. This is because it is unreasonable to assume the biblical writers were being ironic, given that their primary audience was unsophisticated and uneducated in rhetoric.

Have a Meaningful Life & Obtain Eternal Life

Like it or not, we are all going to die one day. But before we do, we want our lives to mean something. We want to leave a positive and lasting legacy to humanity so that we lived a life of meaning.

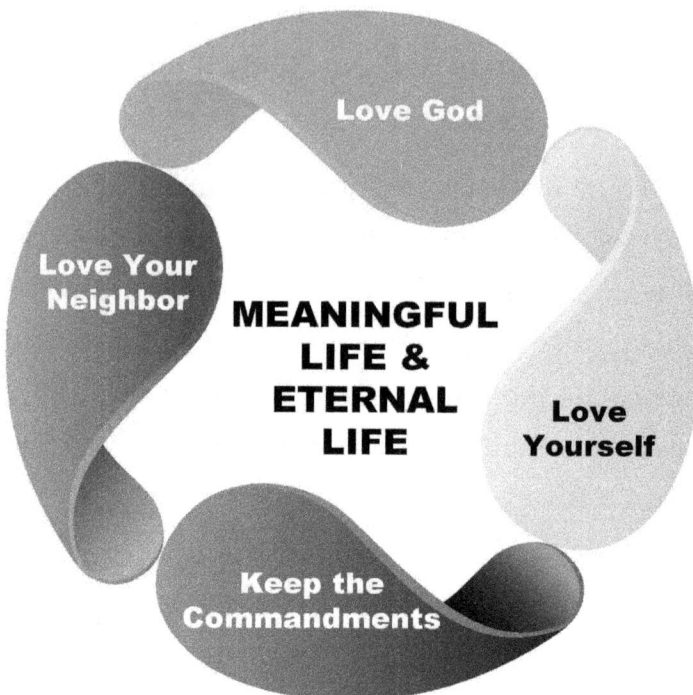

The easiest way to get such a life is to have a family and raise children in truth and righteousness. And the path that Christ outlined is the best, by far, of any way that leads to a joyful life:

- Love God
- Love your neighbor
- Love yourself
- Keep God's commandments

Christ's path may seem simple, but walking on it is profound and the wisest thing we can do. The older we get, the truer his words become.

Think of the big picture: You exist. You think, therefore, you are. After recognizing that you exist, consider how you want to live your life. What worldview provides the best *return on investment* in your effort to validate your self-worth? Nihilism? Hedonism? Narcissism? Atheism?

I urge you to consider Christianity because of how effective its worldview is in giving you a life of meaning.

Important!

The footnotes below reference over a hundred biblical passages to prove this book's depiction of Christ and his followers. Please use your bible or online parallel bibles to confirm the citations are correct. After doing so, consider what the different doctrinal "jigsaw puzzle pieces" look like when combined. You will then see that this book does not exaggerate what God's adopted heirs become, given what we know about the universe.

Christianity teaches your value is incalculable. **Your true worth is vastly greater than any world or even galaxy** since the Creator of the universe,[1] the same entity who created *trillions* of galaxies with each containing *trillions* of worlds, gave up his glory,[2] became human,[3] and suffered[4] and died[5] so that you get the chance of "eternal life" where you share in everything he enjoys with his Father.

The Creator's actions become intelligible because the Holy Bible provides a glimpse of the astonishing fate of those who follow Christ no matter what. They will become the "Children of

---

[1] John 1:3,10,14; Colossians 1:13-17; Hebrews 1:8-12; Hebrews 2:10; 1 Corinthians 8:6; Hebrews 1:2-3; Revelation 3:14.

[2] Philippians 2:5-8; 2 Corinthians 8:9; Hebrews 2:9.

[3] John 1:14; 1 John 4:2-3; 2 John 1:7; Romans 8:3; John 3:16; 1 John 1:1-2; Romans 1:3; 1 Corinthians 15:21; Galatians 4:4; Philippians 2:7-8.

[4] Isaiah 53:6-11; Acts 26:23; Hebrews 5:7-9; 1 Peter 1:11.

[5] John 10:15,17-18; John 17:19; Romans 5:6-8; 1 Corinthians 15:3; 2 Corinthians 5:14-15; Galatians 2:20-21; 1 Thessalonians 5:9-10; Hebrews 2:9-10; Hebrews 9:15,26-28.

God"[6] who are "adopted" by the Father.[7] They share in God's divine nature,[8] oneness,[9] and mutual-indwelling.[10] They will become God's heirs[11] and his Son's fellow-heirs[12] in ruling over the universe.[13]

---

[6] John 1:12-13; 1 John 2:29-3:3; 1 John 3:9; 1 John 5:1-5; Revelation 21:7; Romans 8:14-21; Galatians 3:26-4:7; Hebrews 2:10-17.

[7] Romans 8:15,22-23; Galatians 3:26-4:7; Ephesians 1:4-5.

[8] Romans 8:28-30; 1 Corinthians 1:9; 1 Corinthians 15:48-49; 2 Corinthians 3:18; 2 Corinthians 8:9; Ephesians 3:19; Ephesians 4:13,15,24; Colossians 2:9-10; Colossians 3:10; Hebrews 3:14; Hebrews 12:9-10; 2 Peter 1:3-4; 1 John 1:3-7; 1 John 2:29-3:3.

[9] John 15:1-11; John 17:11,21-23; Romans 8:16-17; 1 Corinthians 6:17; Galatians 3:26-29.

[10] John 6:56; John 14:20,23; John 17:11,21-23; 1 John 5:20; Romans 8:9-11; 1 Corinthians 3:16-17; Galatians 2:20; Ephesians 1:4; Colossians 1:27.

[11] Acts 20:32; Acts 26:18; Romans 8:16-18; Galatians 3:29-4:7; Ephesians 1:11-18; Colossians 1:12-13; Colossians 3:24; Titus 3:7; Hebrews 1:14; Hebrews 9:15; James 2:5; 1 Peter 1:3-5; Revelation 21:7.

[12] Romans 8:17.

[13] Jesus inherits the universe (Matthew 11:27; John 3:35; Ephesians 1:22; Hebrews 1:2; Hebrews 2:10; Matthew 28:18; John 13:3; Romans 9:5; 1 Corinthians 15:27; Colossians 1:16-

They will also share in God's very glory.[14]

God's motivations and his Son's actions create a path that has a destination of staggering glory:

You can become the Creator's fellow-heir in ruling over the universe.

Think about what this means – the scale and grandeur – and what is required to obtain such an eternal reward. Furthermore, consider the fact that the greater the reward, the harder the tasks needed to triumph.

If Christianity's core message is true, then its worldview is the most gratifying perspective one

---

20; John 16:15; John 17:10).

Jesus then shares his inheritance with the Children of God (Luke 12:44; Romans 8:32; 1 Corinthians 3:21-23; 2 Corinthians 6:10; Hebrews 3:14; 2 Timothy 2:12; Revelation 3:21; Revelation 20:4; Luke 12:32; Luke 22:29-30; Ephesians 2:5-7; James 2:5; Revelation 1:6; Revelation 5:10; Revelation 22:5; 2 Timothy 4:7-8; James 1:12; 1 Peter 5:4).

[14] John 17:22; Romans 5:2; Romans 8:17; Colossians 3:4; 2 Timothy 2:10; 2 Peter 1:3-4; Romans 8:17-21,28-30; Romans 9:23-24; 2 Corinthians 4:17; Ephesians 1:11-18; Colossians 1:27; 1 Thessalonians 2:12; 2 Thessalonians 2:13-14; Hebrews 2:10.

can have because we already know the start of our journey, the destination, and the path to tread. We see where the guardrails are that stop us from ignorantly plunging to our doom. There is even a handrail (the Word of God) that we can grasp onto so that we can continue moving forward when the fog of temptation blocks our view of the path. We need to knowingly and intentionally let go of the rail and step over the guardrails (God's commandments) to leave the one and only path that leads to eternal life.

But even if the Christian message is untrue – suppose the whole thing is a fantasy, and another worldview is the correct one – you will still enjoy living as Christ's disciple because the behavior he outlined (love God, your neighbor, and yourself) is the only <u>guaranteed</u> way to having a life of meaning and joy. This is because the behavior satisfies our core nature as beings who, deep down, want to be "good" and do good. We want to love and be loved. We want to belong to something greater than ourselves.

> *No other religion has a higher view of your innate value than Christianity. No other faith has a more appealing view of your eternal fate*

> *than Christianity. No other belief has a greater practical application in giving you a meaningful and joyful life than Christianity.*

If you are human, you possess the same underlying urges and motivations that we all have. You may not see it while you are still young, but wisdom starts to creep in as you mature and experience the good and bad that life offers. Things that were important in your teens and twenties become insignificant in your fifties and above.

The "Obey and Love" Key to a Meaningful Life

Christianity allows you to sense true reality and your incredible destiny as God's heir if you are strong enough and stubborn enough to stay on the path that leads to eternal life.

The Christian worldview has an altruistic God who wants us to obtain eternal happiness without him gaining any advantage from our obedience. Unlike the motivations of the false gods of our past that still live in our entertainment, God does not feed off our sacrifice and prayers. He does not gain additional strength or powers from adoration. Neither does he consume the souls of his followers.

Instead, the Christian God's motivation for us to obey him is a desire for progeny – he wants to "adopt" us as his heirs who will share in his Son's eternal rule over the universe. Our very nature will become compatible with his so we can share in the oneness and glory he shares with his Son.

What the Father, Son, and Holy Spirit are by nature, the Father wants us to become by grace. And he has the will and power to make it happen. [15]

The Christian concept of God is of a being who completely loves us and wants us to be truly happy. And he knows that this can only occur when we become compatible with his nature whereby we, as beings of love, become one and mutually indwell with him, the God of love.

---

[15] Christianity considers you, individually, to be worth more to God than an entire galaxy because he can always make more universes. God's greatest desire is to have Sons and Daughters who freely and willingly transform to share his nature and being. You are his glory, not the universe.

But to become compatible with God, we must consciously choose to live in the specific way he outlined. These "commandments" function as guardrails that alert us to dangers that can destroy us. If we cross them or "break" the commandments, we exit the path and will never reach its destination.

> *God never forces us to obey. Instead, he gives us the freedom to obey or disobey willingly. But there are consequences to our choices that cannot be altered.*

If God is rational, then he gives commandments for a reason. Even if we do not understand those reasons or think they are stupid, the smart thing is to assume God gives them because they help us somehow.

You cannot become a doctor or professional in any field without following specific instructions and a code of ethics. Similarly, neither can you presume to become God's heir without obedience to his imposed rules. And God's conditions would be more stringent than becoming a doctor since the outcome—sharing oneness and glory as God's heir who will rule over the universe beneath Christ—is vastly more significant than any doctor.

Consequently, it is reasonable to assume God's commandments are designed to help us, not him. He is already perfect; we are commanded to become perfect (Matthew 5:48). He is already a God of love; he gives us commandments to become people of love. We benefit from obedience.

God gives commandments to help us become *compatible* with him so that we can have eternal glory as the Children of God who become his Son's fellow-heirs in ruling over the universe forever.

When we examine the New Testament, it becomes evident that each of God's commandments has at least one purpose:

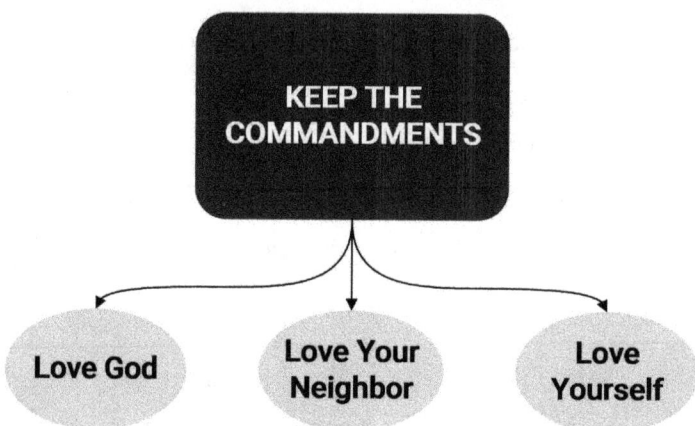

God's commandments are designed to help you love him, your neighbor, and yourself, individually or collectively. Their purpose is for you to:

- **Love God** – To become compatible with the God of love so that you can enjoy the blessings of sharing in his divine nature, oneness, and mutual indwelling.

- **Love your neighbor** – To develop charity and the other moral attributes necessary to become compatible with God and others.

- **Love yourself** – To establish the dignity, self-respect, and steadfastness necessary to become worthy of God's adoption.

For example:

1 John 4:20-21 Those who say, "I love God," but hates their brother or sister is a liar. Those who do not love others, whom they see, cannot love God whom they have not seen. 21 And we have this commandment from him: Those who love God must also love others.

We cannot love God if we do not also love our neighbor. But can we love our neighbor if we lack charity by urging them to keep God's commandments even when they insist on living in a way God condemns? Can we really love someone without telling them the truth for fear of offending them? Is not their eternal fate as the glorified rulers of the universe more important than their feelings during the few years they have on earth?

This attitude is significant from a tangible perspective because we also find meaning and joy in our lives when we strive to bring others onto the path that leads to eternal life. We experience joy when we help them find joy by obeying God. *It is not hypocritically judging others to want to help them become the glorified rulers of the universe.* But we cannot pretend that God's commandments are not there for a reason.

So, live as a person who loves, continually repents, and follows God's commandments. This attitude and behavior keep you on the path, inside the guardrails. Then you can help pull others over the guardrails so that you can walk the path together that leads to eternal life.

Judge without hypocrisy to righteously judge those who need help—and then help them.

> *Matthew 7:1-5 Do not judge, so that you will not be judged. 2 <u>You will be judged with the same standard that you judge others; you will be measured with the same measure you use on others</u>. 3 Why do you see the splinter in another's eye but do not notice the beam in your eye? 4 Or how can you say to another, "Let me take the splinter out of your eye" when you have a beam in your eye? 5 You hypocrite! First remove the beam out of your eye. Then you will be able to see clearly to remove the splinter out of another's eye.*

Christianity's Relevance Checkpoint

Jesus Christ's influence on the world is much more significant than any other person and vastly more than you think. Moreover, his influence goes far beyond morality.

There is a reason why Christianity's worldview has been the most successful mindset in history and why it has utterly improved the human condition (see Part 1: Jesus Christ and His Importance). Even those who did not believe in its message about Christ still lived according to his moral teachings because centuries of experience show they work and produce the best living conditions.

When Christians started applying his teachings to how nations should be run, they quickly created the greatest civilization in history, developed the modern STEM[16] world (which has made everyone's life tangibly better), and conceived of the idea of natural rights – our most important rights.

---

[16] Science, Technology, Engineering, and Mathematics.

To say it another way:

What made the West the most attractive civilization in history, with millions migrating to it every year?

It is because Western nations applied Jesus Christ's teachings to various extents (such as innate natural rights, human dignity, reciprocal empathetic empathy, and the rule of law), which made them appealing to anyone who wants a better life for themselves and their families.

Western civilization used to be proud to be Christian since the benefits the faith provided were enormous and blatant compared to the rest of the world.[17] Churches were always packed,

---

[17] This does not mean everything was great in the West. But

constantly competed with other faiths, and regularly sent out missionaries by the thousands to distant lands to help bring people to Christ.

But since the mid-twentieth century, Western churches lost their zeal and grew silent. They ignored Christ's command to preach the Gospel to all the world and make converts. Timidity, shame, and compromise with ever-changing social trends became the norm. The result was inevitable: Previously vibrant and successful churches emptied and became shadows of what they were. Followers were replaced by placeholders; warriors by wimps.

At the time of this writing, three, perhaps four generations within many Western nations have never attended Christian worship services. As a result, they have never known or appreciated the power, dignity, comfort, and joy Christ brings to the person who strives to follow him. The disparity is stark between towering geniuses like Newton, Euler, Leibniz, and others who viewed

---

compared to *everywhere else at the time*, living in the West was significantly better for the majority, especially for those who were not part of the society's elite.

Christ with wonder and awe and the current celebrities and academics that dismiss him without thought.

Christianity's fall from grace in the West is stunning:

> *The descendants of the faith that, with little effort, defeated the Roman, Greek, Norse, Aztec, Maya, Inca, and other pagan gods now run away from know-it-all college kids with their dyed hair and soy lattes.*

> *The only organization that became the world's sole global power that simultaneously dominated <u>four</u> continents for centuries no longer has real secular influence anywhere on Earth.*

It took over seventeen centuries to finally apply Christ's moral teachings to running nations, which resulted in the emergence of the greatest civilization in history. But Christianity's retreat has come before the full benefits of living on top of Christ's morality have seeped into our consciousness. We have not yet matured as a species to establish our own morality that is as equitable, just, and good as what Christ taught us. Inescapably, we *need* Christ and his teachings.

Christianity's absence from our day-to-day lives made us lose our primary identity that held an ideal behavior that, if followed, directly made our lives and the lives of those around us better. The best of us used to be Christians first and showed it through our actions.

Look at what replaced Christianity's dominance over the average person:

- Spirituality without religion – An idea without sacrifice and genuine effort. It focuses on the internal instead of the external (such as freely serving others). It ignores the fact that Jesus created an organized Church that people join by baptism—the public demonstration of obedience to Christ's command. He called the Church his "Bride," whom he would "marry" on the Last Day. One needs to be part of his Bride's body to enjoy the blessings of eternal life.

- Consumerism – An obsession with material things and services that have no lasting value, such as electronics, apparel, entertainment, and social media.

- Hedonism – An obsession with seeking pleasure such as through sex, food, drugs, alcohol, tattoos, and body modification.

- Atheism – A belief system that claims to be founded on reason but paints its followers into a logical corner by ignoring empirical evidence for God[18] and disregarding the fact that Christ's moral teachings are needed to justify natural rights.[19]

- Rival religions – Both ancient and modern, none of whom possess a morality comparable to what Christ taught, where

---

[18] Testable evidence for God includes the causes of the universe, life, anatomically modern humans with our over forty unique traits, the New Testament as a frameless, unharmonized, correlative anthology, and the Book of Mormon's dictation of dozens of argumentative essays.

[19] Natural rights, such as our rights to life, liberty, and physical security, cannot be morally justified without being placed on Christ's teachings since nothing objective validates them. They violate humanity's nature that values insiders over outsiders. Our innate nature explains why slavery existed and why we have been killing "outsiders" since we lived in bands and tribes despite the victims being equally human.

the weakest outsider has equal worth to the most powerful insider.

The loss of Christian mores in our society sees the return of our human nature's default value, where one only thinks of themself instead of serving others, where one refuses to tolerate differences and consider alternative views, where one ignores the natural rights of opponents and wields force for compliance, where one's beliefs override objective truths, and where insiders are more valuable than outsiders. Tyranny reemerges, rights are again abused, and justice becomes two-tiered, where the rich, powerful, and connected get away with their crimes.

We must stop our world's plunge into the abyss waiting for us since none of us shall enjoy the consequences of a civilizational collapse. And that collapse is inevitable unless we join forces and regain the moral values that our ancestors possessed that made them create the greatest civilization in history.

The default of our nature is terrifying, especially to those who have known no other life than the modern West with its artificially supported floor that raises the public above our core nature. If we do not stop the damage done to our civilization's moral foundation and it collapses, then we will experience the terror, suffering, and death that our ancestors experienced everywhere before Christian morality made humanity's life better.

This is not an exaggeration. Historical facts show life was terrible for everyone, especially those at the bottom of the social classes, compared to living in the modern West. Starvation, disease, and violence were rampant. Half of all children died before their fifth birthday. The average life expectancy was less than forty, slaves were everywhere, and women were property.

An unemployed welfare recipient today has a much better life than a king centuries ago.

We cannot allow our civilization to collapse but must work to improve it. And that is done by underpinning its foundation by discovering or rediscovering Jesus Christ and following him. We must stand up and be seen and heard.

So, join me in telling the world:

I am a Christian! Jesus is my Lord, and I vow to follow him despite my flaws, sins, and failures. His teachings justified our natural rights. His followers created the modern STEM world. He told us the secret to a life of meaning, which is to love God, your neighbor, yourself, and keep the commandments. His name is above all names, and he is Lord of all.

We do not need to belong to the same church to come together and resist evil. Our faiths can have different interpretations and opposing authority claims while jointly worshiping Christ. What unites us—Jesus Christ—is greater than what divides us. Good and smart people can disagree, and that is perfectly fine.

If you do not have a church, there are many to choose from. My church, The Church of Jesus Christ of Latter-day Saints,[20] is the largest denomination in the Latter-day Saint branch of Christianity (over 98% of adherents), but the other four Christian branches (Roman Catholic,[21]

---

[20] https://www.churchofjesuschrist.org

[21] https://www.vatican.va/content/vatican/en.html

Eastern Christian,[22] Anglican/Independent Catholic,[23] and Protestant[24]) also worship Jesus as our Savior. Find a church that shares your values and beliefs, and change churches if you are unhappy with the one you are in.

You deserve the happiness that Jesus gives, and become someone who thoroughly loves so that when you die, you can unite with the God of love (1 John 4:16-17). Live or abide in Christ (John 15:7) and be at peace, no matter what happens.

Finally, your descendants also deserve to live in a world where their natural rights are respected – and that can only occur when the world establishes and enforces laws built on Christ's moral teachings.

---

[22] http://www.patriarchia.ru/en/; https://www.goarch.org/; http://www.ethiopianorthodox.org/; etc.

[23] https://anglicancommunion.org/; etc.

[24] https://www.lutheranworld.org/; https://www.sbc.net/; http://wcrc.ch/; https://worldmethodistcouncil.org/; https://www.pwfellowship.org/; https://pcusa.org/; etc.

Part 1: Jesus Christ and His Importance

Jesus Made Your Life Better

Jesus Christ is the founder of the Christian faith, the world's largest religion. His moral teachings are the foundation of Western civilization and are why you enjoy natural rights. The application of his teachings resulted in the establishment of the Christian milieu, which created, sustained, financed, promoted, and rewarded those who built the modern STEM world that has drastically improved the human condition. Belief in him was the glue that caused hundreds of groups to band together and create the nations of Europe and the Americas.

This means Jesus has positively influenced your life, even if you live in a country that is not Christian and have never heard the Christian message.

You Have Natural Rights Thanks to Jesus Christ's Moral Teachings

If you grew up in a "civilized" country, you know that you possess "rights" that the state and others cannot violate without consequence. Chief among these are your rights to life (no one has the moral right to kill you without just cause), liberty (no one has the moral right to imprison you without just cause), and physical security (no one has the moral right to harm your body). These are examples of "Natural Rights" – rights you have just for being human. No government gave them to you; good governments *recognize* you have them and respect them accordingly.

Natural rights are your most important rights. They are reciprocal – they make you and your worse enemy equal. They make the weakest outsider equal to the most powerful insider.

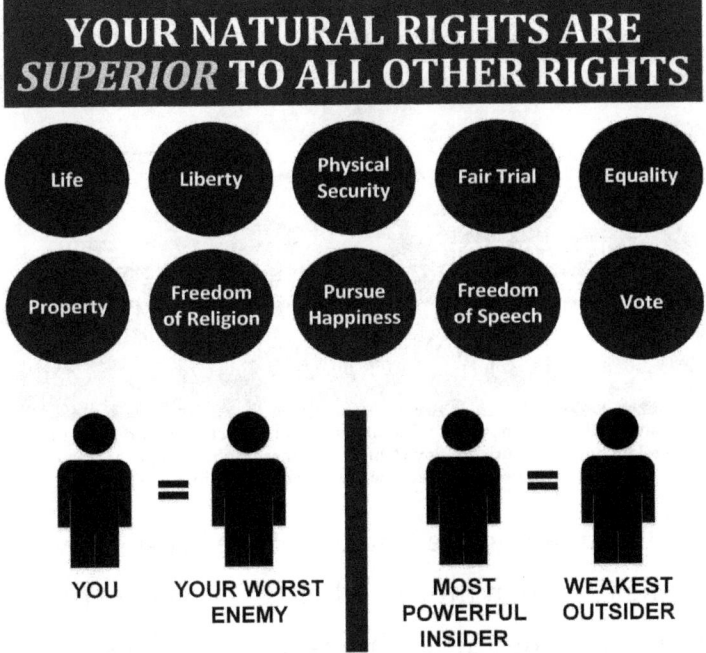

If a right isn't reciprocal, then it isn't a natural right.

However, there is a reason why no nation or culture in history recognized innate natural rights before the West did in the 18th century: **Nothing _objective_ justifies them.** It is a building that floats on air and needs a foundation to validate its existence.

32 | This is Jesus Christ

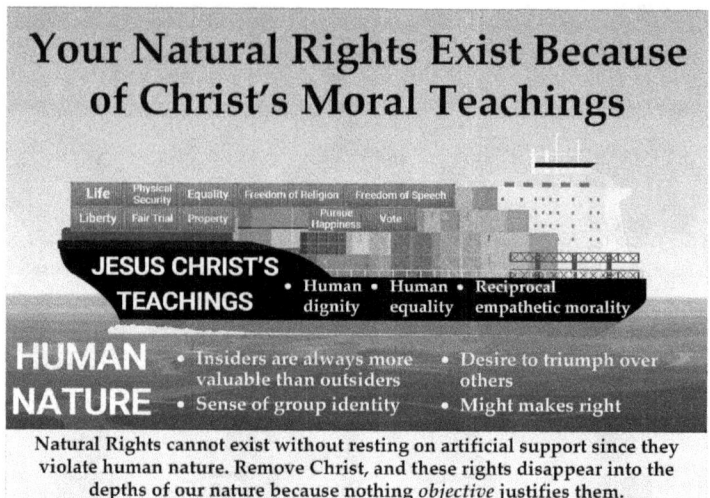

Natural Rights cannot exist without resting on artificial support since they violate human nature. Remove Christ, and these rights disappear into the depths of our nature because nothing *objective* justifies them.

Fortunately, the framers of the West grew up in the Christian milieu, where they were exposed to Christ's moral teachings all their lives. Their culture's highest moral standard aligned with Christ's teachings of empathetic morality (do unto others what you want to be done to yourself), innate human dignity (all are children of God), and human equality (the least of humanity is equal to the king). These moral values were used to justify natural rights.

> *We hold these truths to be <u>self-evident</u>, that all men are created equal, that they are endowed by their Creator with certain unalienable*

Rights, that among these are Life, Liberty and the pursuit of Happiness.[1]

It is easy to prove natural rights' reliance on Christ's moral teachings by asking, *How did the US Founding Fathers know that the unalienable rights to "Life, Liberty, and the pursuit of Happiness" are "self-evident"?* After all, these natural rights are not self-evident in nature, which values insiders over outsiders. This is why you will always save the life of your young child over a stranger's a hundred times out of a hundred. This explains why slavery has existed since time immemorial and why we have been killing "outsiders" for thousands of years. So, what, exactly, makes these rights "self-evident"?

Nothing except Christ's words.

Try a thought experiment. Imagine what kind of life you would have if your natural rights were not respected. A world where the powerful can kill, imprison, or torture you whenever they feel like it. A time when the rulers could take your wife, children, and property just because they

---

[1] Preamble to the US Declaration of Independence (July 4, 1776).

wanted to. A place where the king decides your religion and what type of job you will do for the rest of your life.

That terrible existence has been the reality for most of humanity since we first began. *That was normal, everywhere, for thousands of years.* And it would have continued uninterrupted were not for Christians leveraging Christ's moral teachings to envision and establish natural rights as supreme law just a few centuries ago. Fortunately, that superior morality has now spread to many nations, elevating the quality of life of billions.

Development of Natural Rights

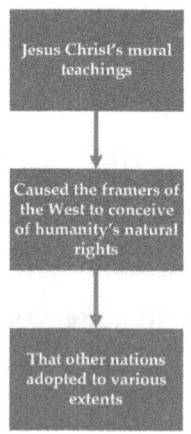

Jesus Christ's moral teachings

↓

Caused the framers of the West to conceive of humanity's natural rights

↓

That other nations adopted to various extents

{

"Do unto others what you want to be done to yourself." (Matthew 7:12)

"Whatever you did to the most unimportant of my brothers and sisters, you did it to me ... Whatever you did not do to the most unimportant of my brothers and sisters, you did not do it to me." (Matthew 25:40,45)

"Love your neighbor as you love yourself." (Mark 12:31)

"Love one another." (John 13:34)

"There is no Jew or Gentile, slave or free, or male or female: You are all one in Christ Jesus." (Galatians 3:28)

All humans have reciprocal natural rights that cannot be morally violated without warrant

So, if your life is better than it could have been without natural rights, then be grateful to Christ and his teachings. You are in his debt.

The Modern STEM World is a Product of Jesus Christ's Moral Teachings

Christ's influence for good was much more than giving humanity our natural rights. His teachings caused his followers to create hospitals, universities, public education, vaccines, and nearly all modern science, technology, engineering, and mathematics. His morality resulted in the abolition and criminalization of slavery, torture, infanticide, human sacrifice, cannibalism, pedophilia, and rape. His followers gave us universal literacy, standardized textbooks, education degrees, academic accreditation, banks, sanitation systems, mass production, modern medicine, intellectual property rights, separation of church and state, and much more.

In other words, it is not an exaggeration to say:

Jesus Christ has a pivotal influence on most <u>tangible</u> things that makes our lives nicer and worth living.

When one examines each of the above items' historical development and answers the "who, why, when, where, and how," what becomes apparent is Christian morality's influence behind the motivations.

For example, those who invented the hospital were driven by a desire to alleviate misery and suffering. They applied Christ's Golden Rule to justify the effort and expense associated with establishing hospitals.

The same is visible with the effort to abolish and criminalize slavery, torture, and other evils. Again, Christ's moral teachings were the primary drivers that marginalized them in our world today. After all, *"Do not do unto others what you do not want to be done to yourself."* If you will not appreciate becoming a slave or getting tortured, then do not do it to others, even when you have the power and ability to do so.

It was Christ's morality that justified the powerful man's self-restraint. It is why there is a significant moral difference between a man with a gun choosing not to shoot someone who hits him versus a defenseless man not retaliating to a bully who punches him in the face.

When the powerful man "turns the other cheek" and does not harm those who harmed him, he follows in the footsteps of the most powerful being who ever lived.

We should not ignore history and objective facts. The grandeur and beauty of the modern world only exist because all civilized and developing nations emulated the West. And the West became the most successful and attractive civilization in history because it was built *on* Christian morality.

We Can Lose It All If We Do Not Resist

The world hates Christ despite the benefits his teachings give humanity. Satan and his followers are doing everything in their power to stamp out his influence, even though it is demonstrable that we find joy and meaning by following him.

Pay attention to what is happening around you: Christians are being ridiculed, shamed, silenced, and punished for daring to follow him. Christian values and symbols are being erased and destroyed. Christian churches, scriptures, and figures are defaced, burned, and banned.

The West's moral foundation is getting destroyed. A way of living with a track record of success that is centuries long and produced the greatest civilization in history and the most significant improvement to our quality of life is systematically being dismantled by those who think they know better. Oligarchies are replacing representatives. The reciprocity of natural rights that made a person equal to his worst enemy, that made the weakest outsider equal to the most powerful insider, is being supplanted by rights and laws that are morally inferior to natural rights because they favor one over another for ideological reasons.

The 500-year track record of modern STEM's reliance on objectivity and inductive experimentation that made this period the best in history is being destroyed by those obsessed with race and gender. Suddenly, math is racist; science is sexist. Conservatism – the mindset that keeps bridges standing, planes flying, and food safe – is now an intolerable evil that must be eliminated by an ever-moving subjectivity based on personal beliefs and feelings.

We are in grave danger. If these people succeed in eliminating the Christian foundation of Western civilization, then there will be nothing to justify our natural rights and representative government. The freedom we have enjoyed will become a distant memory and something our descendants mere decades from now will never experience.

It is time for Christians of every denomination to take a stand. We can no longer continue the Christian apathy that has characterized the past. Instead, we must push back that Christian morality is crucial for our happiness and safety. All humans, regardless of whatever makes us different, have equal value. Every single person has inherent dignity. The Golden Rule's *"Do unto others what you want to be done to yourself; do not do unto others what you do not want to be done to yourself"* is noble and worthwhile.

But to reestablish our Christian moral values effectively, we need to feel that truth within our bones and deep within our gut. To get the conviction that strengthens spines even in the face of terrifying danger and death, we need to understand who Christ is to appreciate the transformative morality he gave the world. Even better, the Holy Spirit can witness to us of him. This happens when we pray and ask God to tell us the truth about Jesus and pay attention to our feelings and impressions afterward.

When the Holy Spirit witnesses to us of Jesus Christ and we recognize that communication for what it truly is—God is speaking directly to us (Spirit-to-spirit)—we can become strong and unyielding. We then know, without a doubt, that we have experienced the divine. That touch brings awe, joy, comfort, and peace that brands our hearts. We then know God is real, for we have felt him and his great love for us. While we can never prove the experience to others or replicate it in a lab, we can live it by changing our behavior and following his Son until the end of our days.

Is Jesus Still Relevant Today?

We like to think we are rational beings who are not governed by emotions and primitive superstitions. We celebrate science and utilize technology to make our lives easier and nicer. Our educational system, media, and popular culture have conditioned us that science, not religion, is the most credible source of information and guidance.

And it is hard to dispute this assertion since it has been science, not religion, that has transformed our world into one that is richer, healthier, and more knowledgeable.

But just throwing out "science" as the catch-all answer to questions does a fundamental disservice to the problems we face as humans. They are not resolved by just citing Ockham's logic; sometimes, the simplest answer is *not* the correct one. This is no different than a person answering every problem with "God wills it."

One does not need to be a Christian to observe the blatantly obvious fact that our society's movement away from Jesus and his teachings has negatively affected our happiness and self-worth.

Despite all our gadgets and entertainment, we have become unmoored, miserable, and lonely. We feel empty and worthless. We desperately want to fill the void inside us with something more meaningful and lasting than sex, substances, and entertainment.

We have forgotten who we are and why we are here.

Jesus did not just bring knowledge; he taught us how to live. That way of life – do unto others what you want to be done to yourself, show love and kindness toward others, treat others as if they were the King himself, forgive those who have wronged you, love your enemies, do good to those who hate you, respect the law and the dignity and rights of others – makes our world a nicer and more enjoyable place to live. Living his teachings results in our relationships becoming better, our marriages and families stronger, our neighborhoods nicer, and our nations happier. But, perhaps most crucially, living his teachings gives meaning and joy to our lives regardless of what life brings.

To be truly happy and content requires living a life of meaning. And Christ showed us that such a life could only be achieved by loving God, our neighbors, ourselves, and keeping God's commandments.

When you live such a life, you become truly happy. You do not need medication, drugs, and loveless sex to find joy in your existence. You find pleasure in life, in service, and in sacrifice.

Our society must pivot back to following Christ to avoid the abyss in front of us. If we care about the future and our children's quality of life, we must stand firm for eternal principles against social forces that dictate new morals. We must not be afraid to be mocked, vilified, and even punished for clinging to outdated views.

We have tried living away from Christ's morality and realize that it does *not* work. It results in us reverting to the default of our nature that values insiders more than outsiders. It makes people unequal and makes our quality of life much worse.

Our world is again sick with moral relativity and a vacuous sense of reality where people seem unable to tell right from wrong. The line between what is real and what is fantasy is so blurred that simple objective facts cannot be said without getting punished. Behaviors once opposed and condemned are now normalized, celebrated, and even sanctified. We have stopped resisting evil out of fear of being labeled and punished.

We cannot continue the path we are on if we want to be happy with ourselves. And Christ provides the answer.

What Jesus Said About Himself

Given Jesus's enormous positive impact on all our lives, we should, at the very least, baseline who he claimed to be. Was he God made flesh or just a prophet or wise teacher?

Jesus claimed:

- He came from the Father and will return to him after he leaves the Earth (John 16:28)

- He was the Father's only Son (John 3:18)

- He possessed glory before the Earth's creation (John 17:5)

- No one can be saved or approach the Father except through him (John 14:6)

- One sees the Father when looking at Jesus (John 14:7-12)

- He is equal to the Father in some manner (John 5:17-18,23)
- He is one with the Father (John 10:30)
- He mutually indwells with the Father (John 14:10-11)
- He expects us to keep his commandments (John 15:10)
- He has the power to forgive us of our sins (Mark 2:10)
- He sits on the Father's right-hand side (Luke 22:69)
- He will return to Earth at the head of a heavenly force (Matthew 25:31)
- He will oversee the replacement of the Earth with an upgraded version (Matthew 19:28)
- The Father gave him the entire universe for an inheritance (John 3:35)
- He will share his inheritance – this universe – with his followers (Luke 22:29-30)
- He will save all humanity from death (John 5:28-29)

- He will judge all humans (John 5:22-30)
- Those who believe in him will receive eternal life (John 3:15-16,36)
- He will share oneness and mutually-indwell with his followers (John 17:11,21-23)
- He will share his glory with his followers (John 17:22)

Would a mere prophet of God say such things? What about a righteous and wise teacher? Of course not. Then there can be no doubt that although Jesus never said straight out that he was "God" in the Bible, he described himself in a manner where the only conclusion is that he was referring to himself as "God." No human, regardless of holiness, can claim what he claimed.

The issue then is that, as C.S. Lewis pointed out, Jesus was either telling the truth (he is "God"), or he was lying or delusional. There are no other options if he was an actual historical figure.

When you ponder his impact on humanity and in your life, who do you think he was?

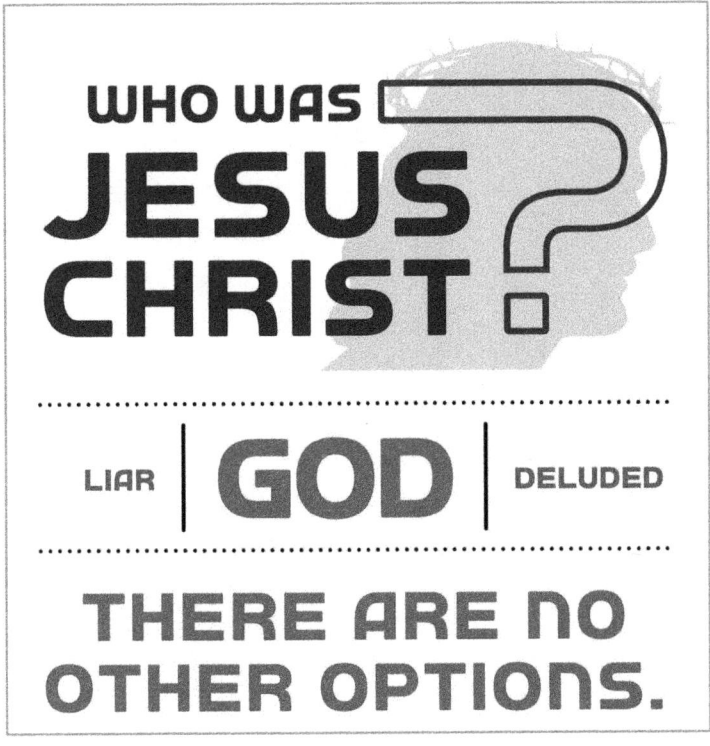

For me, Jesus Christ is *my* God.

Part 2: Understanding Jesus Christ

IMPORTANT!

This book's structure encourages you to *act and not be acted upon* so that you can grow and become happy with who you are. A vital part of loving yourself is taking charge of your life and not relying on others when you can do something on your own. Since your personal beliefs or interpretations of biblical passages have an outsize influence on how you live your life, you are urged to use your free mind to justify your beliefs.

Furthermore, because you are human, you have the absolute right to your beliefs and do not need anyone else to tell you what to think. Regardless of what some uncharitable zealots claim, *God does <u>not</u> care how you interpret his doctrines, only that you honestly strive to follow his Son, obey him, and become like him.* While this book teaches biblical truth, it deliberately leaves the interpretation to you. Feel free to use whatever resources you want (preferably from opposing faiths) to outline how you understand the Bible's passages, but stay the master of your own mind.

Write your beliefs or understandings of what the biblical passages are trying to say in the **Things to Ponder** tables. Underline and highlight the biblical text to help you codify your thoughts. *There are no wrong answers except the opposite of what the texts say.* Date your entries to evaluate your changing views over the years and decades.

It is normal for your understanding to adjust as you age, and life circumstances change. There will be times when you become closer to God and times when you move away from him. By writing down your interpretations during the ebb and flow of life, you give yourself criteria that can be assessed to help you make corrections so that you live a life of meaning and joy regardless of the evil and pain you experience.

So, come, and discover the wonderful Jesus Christ and all he has done for us! I hope that you constantly come closer to our Lord so that by the time you stand before him for judgment, you become one with the God of love because you became a person of love.

Chapter 1: Jesus is "God"

The Bible calls the Father "God" and distinguishes between Jesus and his Father, "God." Jesus is not the entity known as his Father or God. However, the word "God" is also used in the sense of nature or "species" (per our current scientific worldview).

This book refers to Jesus as "God" in the latter sense. Does he belong to the "God" species just as we belong to the *Homo sapiens sapiens* species?

1.1 Jesus Already Existed Before Becoming Human

> *John 1:1-3,10,14 In the beginning was the Word; the Word existed with God; and the Word was God. 2 He existed with God in the beginning. 3 He created the universe. Nothing exists that he did not create ... 10 He went and lived on Earth. And even though he created it, the world's inhabitants did not know who he was ... 14 The Word became flesh and lived among us. We have seen his glory—the glory of the only Son of the Father, full of grace and truth.*

John 8:56-59 *"Your father Abraham was thrilled at the thought of my coming—he saw it and rejoiced."*

57 The Jews then said, "You are not even fifty! Have you seen Abraham?"

58 Jesus then replied, "I am telling you truthfully, before Abraham was even born, I AM!"

59 When they heard this, they picked up rocks to stone him to death, but Jesus hid and slipped out of the temple.

Colossians 1:15-17 *He is the image of the God who has never been seen, and existed before the universe was created. 16 He created the universe. Everything in heaven and earth, everything we see and cannot see, including thrones, powers, rulers, or authorities; he created them all, and they are for him. 17 He existed before the universe and causes it to hold together.*

2 Timothy 1:9-10 *God saved us and called us to a holy life, not because of our works, but because that was his plan and grace using Christ Jesus from before time began. 10 This* *plan is now shown to us by the manifestation of our Savior Jesus Christ, who destroyed death, and brought life and immortality through the gospel.*

1 Peter 1:19-20 *But with the incalculably valuable blood of Christ, the unblemished and spotless Lamb of God, 20 who was chosen before the world was created, and was revealed in these last days for your sake.*

1 John 1:1-2 *The one who existed from the beginning, whom we have personally seen with our own eyes, heard with our own ears, and touched with our own hands—is the Word of Life! 2 (He who is Life itself appeared. We have seen him and testify that he is Eternal Life! He who was with the Father in the beginning was manifested to us!)*

1 John 2:13 *I am writing to you who are long-time members of the faith because you know him who existed from the beginning. I am writing to you who are still young in the faith because you have overcome the evil one.*

Things to Ponder

1. Do the passages say Jesus already existed before birth, or was he only a thought in God's mind?

2. Where did Jesus dwell before his birth? Try to picture that place in your mind – what does it look like to you?

3. Which came first, Jesus or the universe? Why?

4. Why do you think Jesus came to this planet to get a physical body out of all the worlds in the universe?

1.2 Jesus Possessed the "God" Nature Before Becoming Human

John 1:1 *In the beginning was the Word; the Word existed with God; and the Word was God.*

Philippians 2:5-7 *Have the same attitude Jesus Christ had:*

6 Although having the same nature as God, he did not think to forcefully cling to his equality with God, 7 but emptied himself of it, and took upon him the nature of a slave and became human.

Hebrews 1:2-3 *And now, God has spoken to us through his Son in these last days. God has given the universe to him as an inheritance, and created it through him. 3 The Son radiates God's glory and is the exact copy of the very essence of God. He sustains the universe by the power of his word. After he made the purification for sins, he sat down on the right-hand side of the majestic God in heaven!*

2 Corinthians 4:4 *The god of this world has blinded the minds of unbelievers so that they* *cannot see the light of the gospel of the glorious Christ, who is in the image of God.*

Colossians 1:15 *He is the image of the God who has never been seen, and existed before the universe was created.*

Things to Ponder
1. What kind of nature did Jesus have before becoming human? What does that tell you about him and his capabilities?

2. What does it mean when the Bible says the Son is "The exact copy of the very essence of God"?

3. Could Jesus being in the "Image of God" refer to an outward physical appearance, or could it refer to "nature," especially since it was said to be that way already "before the universe was created"?

4. *Think deeper: What was the equality with God that Jesus gave up when he became human if he remained entirely "God" while human? Was it glory and honor, or was it something else?*

> 5. Do John, Paul, and the Hebraist share the same premortal view of Jesus, and was it of him being a greater than human entity? Explain.

1.3 Jesus Possessed "Glory" Before Creation

John 17:5,22,24 Now, Father, glorify me with yourself and restore the glory I shared with you before the world's creation . . . 22 I gave them the glory you gave me so that they may be one just as we are one . . . 24 Father, I want those you gave me to be with me where I am. I want them to see the glory you gave me because you already loved me before the world's creation.

***Philippians 2:6-8** Although having the same nature as God, he did not think to forcefully cling to his equality with God, 7 but emptied himself of it, and took upon him the nature of a slave and became human. 8 As a mortal man, he humbled himself and was so obedient to the Father's will that he stooped to die the utterly degrading death on the cross.*

Things to Ponder
1. What did Jesus have "before the world's creation"? What do you think it means?

2. When Jesus became human, what did he do with the glory that made him equal to God the Father? Why did he do it?

3. What attributes did Christ have that made him give up his glory?

> 4. What do you think Christ means when he said he gives the glory God gave him to his followers? What is the effect on us?

1.4 Jesus Causes the Forces of the Universe to Hold Together

Colossians 1:17 He existed before the universe and causes it to hold together.

Hebrews 1:3 The Son radiates God's glory and is the exact copy of the very essence of God. He sustains the universe by the power of his word. After he made the purification for sins, he sat down on the right-hand side of the majestic God in heaven!

Things to Ponder

1. What is Jesus continually doing to the universe? Why do you think he is doing it?

2. Do these passages explain why the universe seems fine-tuned for the emergence of life? Why?

3. Do Paul and the Hebraist both describe Jesus as being the active source of the universe's fundamental integrity? Why do you think they described it in the present tense and not past tense?

4. *Expand your mind. What would happen to any region of space, such as the volume of a world, star, or entire galaxy, if Jesus decided not to support the universe's fundamental forces in that region? Why?*

5. *Think of the consequences of having total active control over the universe's structure. Can Christ create worlds? Can he create galaxies? Can he command matter to change from one element to another? Can he create stellar megastructures? Explain.*

> 6. What do you think will happen to the universe if Christ stops supporting its fundamental forces? Why?

1.5 Jesus Was Called "God"

Matthew 4:7 Jesus replied, "It is also written that you shall not put the Lord your God to the test."

John 1:1 *In the beginning was the Word; the Word existed with God; and the Word was God.*

John 1:18 *No one has ever seen God; he has been revealed by the only God who is at the Father's side.*

John 20:28 *Thomas exclaimed to him, "My Lord and my God!"*

Acts 20:28 *Guard yourselves and the flock that the Holy Spirit entrusted to you. Feed the church of God, which he paid for with his own blood.*

2 Thessalonians 1:12 *So that the name of our Lord Jesus may be glorified in you and you in him, according to the grace of our God and Lord Jesus Christ.*

Titus 2:13 *Looking for the blessed hope and manifestation of the glory of the great God and Savior Jesus Christ.*

Hebrews 1:8-10 *But to the Son, he said: "Your throne, O God, will last forever. You rule your kingdom with a scepter of righteousness. 9 You have loved righteousness and hated wickedness. Therefore, O God, your*

God, has anointed you with the oil of joy above anyone else. 10 And in the beginning, you, Lord, laid the foundation of the earth. Your hands created the heavens."

2 Peter 1:1 *Simon Peter, a servant and apostle of Jesus Christ, writing to those who share the same precious faith through the righteousness of Jesus Christ, our God and Savior.*

1 John 5:20 *We know the Son of God came and gave us understanding so that we may know him who is true. We are in him who is true — in his Son, Jesus Christ. He is the True God and is life eternal.*

Things to Ponder
1. Who was Satan tempting? Why did Christ say such a thing to Satan? Who was he to Satan?

Jesus is "God" | 73

2. *Who was the God on the Father's side?*

3. *To whom was Thomas speaking? Did Christ correct him? Why not?*

74 | This is Jesus Christ

4. Who was this God who paid for the church with his own blood?

5. What word did God the Father use to address the Son? If the Father calls the Son that word, can we?

Jesus is "God" | 75

6. *Who is "our God and Savior" according to Peter? Who is "the True God and is life eternal" according to John?*

7. *Are these six biblical authors describing Jesus in greater-than-human terms? Why did they do so?*

8. Based on the above biblical passages, who is "our God"? Explain the implications and consequences of viewing Jesus Christ as "our God," keeping in mind that Jesus said whoever honors him honors the Father (John 5:23), and they are "one" and mutually indwell in one another in some manner (John 10:30,38; John 14:10-11,20; John 17:11,21,23; 2 Corinthians 5:19).

> 9. Do the passages that call or describe Jesus to be "God" mean he is the same person as the Father, or do they mean he has the "God" nature?

1.6 Jesus Had the "God" Nature Within His Physical Body

Colossians 1:19 God was pleased that all his fullness dwelt in Jesus.

Colossians 2:9 All of God's fullness dwells in the body of Jesus.

Things to Ponder

1. *What dwelt in the physical body of Jesus? What do you think it means?*

2. *What kind of being can contain all of God's "fullness" in his body? Why wasn't it limited?*

> 3. Why do you think it was essential for God's fullness to be within Christ's physical body?

1.7 Jesus Had Mutual Indwelling and "Oneness" With the Father

John 10:38 But if I do the work, even though you do not believe me, at least believe the works, so that you will know that the Father is in me, and I am in him.

John 13:31-32 After he had left, Jesus said, "The time has come for the Son of Man's glorification, and God is glorified in him. 32 If God is glorified in him, God will glorify the

Son of Man within himself, and shall immediately glorify him."

John 14:10-11,20 Do you not believe that I am in the Father, and the Father is in me? The words I say are not from me but from the Father who dwells in me.

11 Believe me when I say I am in the Father and the Father is in me or at least believe because of my work . . . 20 On that day, you will understand that I am in my Father, and you are in me, and I am in you.

2 Corinthians 5:19 God was in Christ and was reconciling the world to himself by not holding humanity's sins against them. He has given us the message of reconciliation.

John 10:30 The Father and I are one.

John 17:11,21-23 Holy Father, I am about to leave this world and go to you, but they are staying in this world. Protect them by the power of your name so that they may be one as we are one . . . 21 That they may be one just as you are in me and I in you. May they be in us so that the world may believe that you sent me. 22 I gave them the glory you gave me so that *they may be one just as we are one. 23 I in them and you in me, so that they may become perfectly united. The world will then know that you sent me and loved them just as you loved me.*

Things to Ponder
1. Who was Jesus claiming dwelt within him? What does this imply about their relationship?

2. Who did people see when they gazed upon Jesus? Why do you think that is?

3. Who did Jesus have "oneness" with? Look closer: he had oneness with more than just one. What does that bi-directional oneness mean to you?

4. *In your own words, what benefits are there to having oneness and mutual indwelling with God? Now, and in the next life?*

1.8 Jesus Gave Up His Glory to Become Human

John 17:5 Now, Father, glorify me with yourself and restore the glory I shared with you before the world's creation.

Philippians 2:5-8 Have the same attitude Jesus Christ had:

6 Although having the same nature as God, he did not think to forcefully cling to his equality with God, 7 but emptied himself of it, and took upon him the nature of a slave and became human. 8 As a mortal man, he humbled himself and was so obedient to the Father's will that he stooped to die the utterly degrading death on the cross.

2 Corinthians 8:9 You know the grace of our Lord Jesus Christ: Although he was rich, he became poor for your sakes, so that you may become rich through his poverty.

Hebrews 2:9 Jesus was temporarily made lower than angels. He is now crowned with glory and honor because he subjected himself to death. By God's grace, he died for everyone!

Jesus is "God" | 85

Hebrews 5:8 *Even though he was God's Son, he learned obedience from the things he suffered.*

Things to Ponder
1. What did Jesus give up when he became human? Why would he do that?
2. Why did Jesus become human?

3. For whom did Jesus die? Why would he do that?

4. What did Jesus learn from his suffering? Why is that important?

Chapter 2: Jesus is the "Son of God"

The Bible calls Jesus the "Son of God" dozens of times because of two doctrines: Jesus was a product of a miraculous pregnancy, and he possessed a unique relationship with God *before* becoming human. It was *not* because he taught "righteousness," or because he was "holy" and had special wisdom, or because he became "enlightened."

2.1 Product of a Miraculous Pregnancy

The Bible claims Jesus's mother, Mary, became pregnant with him by the power of God while still a virgin. In modern genetic terms, this means Mary's haploid ovum merged with something other than a haploid human sperm to become the diploid zygote that became Christ's physical body. And whatever this haploid "sperm" was, it contained the Y chromosome that resulted in a male gender (XY).

No human male sperm contributed half of the 23 paired chromosomes to become the body of Jesus Christ. Instead, God provided that portion of his genome through the Holy Spirit. Whatever that was, it resulted in the "fullness" of God to be within Christ's flesh (Colossians 1:19; Colossians 2:9).

> ***Matthew 1:18-20*** *Now, this is how the birth of Jesus Christ occurred: While his mother, Mary, was engaged to be married to Joseph, she became pregnant by the power of the Holy Spirit while still a virgin. 19 And Joseph, her husband, being a decent man and unwilling to humiliate her publicly, sought to annul their marriage in private. 20 While he was struggling with what to do, an angel of the Lord appeared to him in a dream and said, "Joseph, you son of David. Do not be afraid to keep Mary as your wife because what is conceived in her is from the Holy Spirit!"*

> ***Luke 1:31-35*** *Now listen! You will become pregnant and give birth to a Son and name him Jesus. 32 He shall be great and will be called the Son of the Highest. The Lord God shall give him his forefather David's throne. 33 He shall reign over Jacob's house forever, and his kingdom will never end.*

> *34 Mary then said to the angel, "How is this possible since I have never been intimate with a man?"*

Jesus is the "Son of God" | 89

35 The angel answered, "The Holy Spirit will come upon you, and the power of the Highest will overshadow you. The Holy One who will be born will be called the Son of God."

Things to Ponder
1. What or who caused Mary's pregnancy with Jesus?
2. Did a human male contribute genetic material to the zygote that became the physical body of Jesus? If no, then who was his biological father?

3. *Since pregnancy occurs when a sperm and egg cell fuse to create a zygote that is implanted in the womb and numerous artificial techniques exist that can result in pregnancy without sexual intercourse (e.g., IVF, ICSI, artificial insemination), was a sex act needed for Mary to become pregnant?*

4. *Why was Jesus called the "Son of God"?*

> 5. *How do you think the Holy Spirit did it? How was the zygote that became Jesus made? (There is no right or wrong answer, just write down your thoughts.)*

2.2 Unique Relationship with God Before Becoming Human

The Bible asserts Jesus had a unique relationship with God, where he lived with God as his "Son" *before* becoming human.

John 1:14 *The Word became flesh and lived among us. We have seen his glory — the glory of the only Son of the Father, full of grace and truth.*

1 John 4:9-10 *God showed his love toward us by sending his only Son into the world so that we might live through him. 10 This is real love: Not that we loved God, but because He loved us — and sent his Son to be the appeasing sacrifice for our sins!*

Romans 8:3,32 *God did what the Law of Moses was incapable of doing due to the weakness of flesh: God condemned sin in the flesh by sending his own Son to become flesh . . . 32 Since God did not spare his own Son but gave him up for our sakes, there is then nothing that he would not also give us.*

Galatians 4:4 *But when the appointed time arrived, God sent his Son, born of a woman, born under the law.*

John 3:13-18 *No one has ever gone up to heaven except he who came down from heaven — the Son of Man. 14 Just as Moses lifted the snake on the pole while in the* *wilderness, so shall the Son of Man be lifted up, 15 so that whoever believes in him shall not perish but have eternal life. 16 God loved humankind so much that he gave up his only Son. Whoever believes in him shall not perish but have eternal life.*

17 God sent his Son to the world not to condemn humankind but to save it through him. 18 No condemnation is done to those who believe in him. But those who refuse to believe are already condemned because they do not believe in the name of God's one and only Son.

John 6:38-39 *God sent me down from heaven to do what he wants, not what I want. 39 When he sent me to earth, he wanted me to keep all those he gave me and elevate them on the last day.*

John 8:42 *Jesus said to them, "If God were your Father, you would love me because I came from God. I am not here on my own accord—he sent me."*

Things to Ponder

1. Was Jesus already God's "Son" before he was sent to Earth? What does that tell you about his unique relationship with the Father?

2. Why did God send his Son to Earth?

Jesus is the "Son of God" | 95

> 3. *Think deeper: Why was it necessary for God's Son to become human to save us instead of having an all-powerful, all-good God merely exert his power to remove our sins?*

4. Was there something unique about Jesus being God's only "Son"? If so, what do you think it was?

Chapter 3: Jesus is Human

According to the Bible, Jesus was a man. He was born, cried, bled, got hungry, showed emotions, and displayed all of humanity's characteristics. But he was different in two crucial ways: He lived in a manner where he never sinned (2 Corinthians 5:21; Hebrews 4:15; Hebrews 7:26; Hebrews 9:14; 1 Peter 2:22; 1 John 3:5), and he was also fully "God" while being fully "man."

3.1 God (Jesus Christ) Became Human

John 1:14 The Word became flesh and lived among us. We have seen his glory—the glory of the only Son of the Father, full of grace and truth.

1 John 4:2-3 This is how you will know the Spirit of God: Every spirit that acknowledges Jesus Christ came in the flesh is of God! 3 Those who do not acknowledge Jesus are not from God. This is the spirit of the antichrist and is already in the world.

2 John 1:7 There are many deceivers in the world who do not acknowledge Jesus Christ came in the flesh. These are deceivers and the antichrist.

Romans 8:3 *God did what the Law of Moses was incapable of doing due to the weakness of flesh: God condemned sin in the flesh by sending his own Son to become flesh.*

Things to Ponder
1. Was Jesus truly human with flesh identical to ours, or was his incarnation just an illusion?
2. Chapter 1 shows Jesus was "God," while Chapter 3 shows he was also human. What does the fusion of both natures in one person mean?

3. *John's pass/fail criterion, "<u>Acknowledge Jesus Christ came in the flesh</u>" explicitly unites "Jesus" with "Christ" in human flesh. So essential is this union within flesh that he says those who refuse to acknowledge it are "antichrist." The divine Christ is <u>not</u> a separate entity from the human Jesus. The divine Christ did <u>not</u> enter and leave the human Jesus.* **They are one and the same.**

   Why is it so important to accept that the Son of God, an entity who is "God" by nature, <u>became</u> human flesh?

4. How should we view those who claim Christ is not the same being as Jesus, especially if they allege that the divine Christ enters and leaves many human bodies over time?

5. What happened to sin caused by our weak flesh when Jesus became flesh? Why?

3.2 The Son of God Became Human (*Homo sapiens sapiens*)

John 3:16 *God loved humankind so much that he gave up his only Son. Whoever believes in him shall not perish but have eternal life.*

1 John 1:1-2 *The one who existed from the beginning, whom we have personally seen with our own eyes, heard with our own ears, and touched with our own hands—is the Word of Life! 2 (He who is Life itself appeared. We have seen him and testify that he is Eternal Life! He who was with the Father in the beginning was manifested to us!)*

Romans 1:3 *Concerning his Son, a literal descendant of David.*

1 Corinthians 15:21 *Since death came because of a man, it is necessary for the resurrection of the dead to also come from a man.*

Galatians 4:4 *But when the appointed time arrived, God sent his Son, born of a woman, born under the law.*

Philippians 2:7-8 *but emptied himself of it, and took upon him the nature of a slave and* *became human. 8 As a mortal man, he humbled himself and was so obedient to the Father's will that he stooped to die the utterly degrading death on the cross.*

Hebrews 2:14-18 *Since God's children are humans with flesh and blood, he, too, shared in that same nature so that by his death, he may annul the devil, who holds the power of death, 15 and liberate those who were in slavery and terrified of death.*

16 He did not come to help the angels; he came to help Abraham's descendants. 17 This is why he needed to fully have the exact human nature as his siblings, so that he may be a merciful and empathetic high priest before God, and offer an authentic sacrifice for the sins of humankind. 18 Because he knows what it is like to suffer when tempted, he can help those who are tempted.

Things to Ponder

1. *Think deeper: If all the fullness of God was in the physical body of Jesus Christ (Colossians 1:19; Colossians 2:9), was the fullness of humanity also within him? In other words, if he was 100% God, was he also 100% human? Explain.*

2. Why did Jesus become human? Provide at least three reasons.

3. By becoming fully human, what did Jesus annul by his death? Why is this important for your eternal future?

> 4. *By becoming fully human, Jesus learned firsthand what it is like to experience temptation, misery, suffering, and pain. Why is this important?*

3.3 As a Human, Jesus Reconciles Us to God

Colossians 1:20-22 And through Jesus, God reconciled the universe to himself, whether things on earth or in the heavens—by making peace through Jesus's blood on the cross.

21 You were once alienated from God, with a hostile mind because of your evil actions. 22 But now, Jesus has reconciled you in his flesh through his death, to present you to God, holy, unblemished, and beyond reproach.

Things to Ponder

1. What did Jesus Christ's Atonement reconcile to God?

2. What did Jesus use to reconcile us to God? Why?

3. *What can happen to us because of the reconciliation?*

4. *Why did Christ's humanity result in our reconciliation with God?*

3.4 Jesus Triumphed as a Human

Revelation 5:5,9,12 And one of the elders said to me, "Do not cry. Look! The Lion of the tribe of Judah, the Root of David, has triumphed and can open the scroll and the seven seals." ... 9 And they sang a new song, saying, "You are worthy to take the scroll and break its seals. For you were slaughtered and used your blood to purchase people unto God out of every tribe, language, ethnicity, and nation." ... 12 They said with a loud voice, "The Lamb who was slaughtered is worthy to receive power, riches, wisdom, strength, honor, glory, and praise!"

Things to Ponder
1. What happened to Jesus, who was called the "Lion of the tribe of Judah, the Root of David" and the "Lamb"?

Jesus is Human | 109

2. What did he use to pay for people?

3. What was he worthy of?

4. Why was Jesus worthy to receive all those blessings?

3.5 Jesus Can Never Experience Death Again

Romans 6:9-10 Know that Christ was resurrected from the dead—he can never experience death again! Death can never again have power over him. 10 When he died, he died once for all time to conquer sin. And the life he lives, he lives for God.

Romans 8:34 Who can condemn? Christ Jesus is the one who died, who rose again, and who is even now on the right-hand side of God interceding for us.

2 Corinthians 5:15 He died for all so that those who live will no longer live for themselves, but for the one who died and rose again.

Things to Ponder
1. Can Jesus Christ ever die again (the separation of the spirit from the physical body – James 2:26)?

Jesus is Human | 111

2. *How often can the entity we know to be the pre-mortal Son of God or Jesus Christ become mortal?*

3. *If Jesus had a <u>physical</u> human body after his resurrection that others could feel, and he could never experience death again, does he currently have an immortal physical body? Will he continue to have it forevermore? Why?*

> 4. *If someone claims to be the returned Jesus or Christ, but he is a mortal human, capable of dying and feeling pain and bodily injury, is it possible for that person to be legitimate, or is he a false Jesus or false Christ? Explain.*

3.6 Jesus Lives Forever with a Physical Body

Revelation 1:18 *I am the living one. I was dead but look at me now—I am alive and will be for all eternity. I hold the keys of Death and Hades.*

Hebrews 7:16 *Jesus became a High Priest, not by belonging to the priestly tribe designated by* *the Law of Moses, but by possessing an indestructible and endless life!*

Matthew 28:8-9 *As they hastily left the tomb with fear and great joy, and were rushing to tell the disciples what the angel instructed, 9 Jesus met them and said, "Greetings!" They then prostrated themselves before him and held on to his feet, and worshiped him.*

Luke 24:36-46 *While they were talking about these things, Jesus suddenly appeared in their midst and said, "May you have peace."*

37 They then jumped in terror and feared they saw a ghost.

38 He said to them, "Why are you frightened? Why are your hearts filled with doubt? 39 Look at my hands and my feet. It is me! Touch me and confirm it is me. A ghost does not have a body of flesh and bone that you see I have."

40 He then showed them his hands and feet. 41 And while they still could not believe it was him out of sheer joy and amazement, he asked them, "Do you have anything to eat?"

42 They then handed him some broiled fish, 43 which he then ate in front of them.

44 He then said, "This is what I told you before—everything about me that is written in the law of Moses, the prophets, and psalms need to be fulfilled." 45 He then opened their minds so that they could completely understand the scriptures, 46 and told them, "This is what was written: 'The Messiah needs to suffer and rise from the dead after three days.

Things to Ponder
1. When Jesus died, he left his physical body and existed as a spirit. When he resurrected, he re-entered his physical body to live again. If he is alive and has an indestructible and endless life, does he have an immortal physical body today?

2. *Could the women feel the feet of the resurrected Jesus? What does this tell you about his immortal body?*

3. *Did the resurrected Jesus have a physical body of flesh and bone that his followers felt with their own hands? What does this tell you about his immortal body?*

> 4. Why do you think it is essential to know Jesus lives again with an immortal physical body? What does this tell you about your immortality after you are resurrected?

3.7 Jesus Made a Single Sacrifice for All Time for All Humans

John 10:15 As the Father knows me, I also know the Father. I lay down my life for the sheep.

Romans 6:10 *When he died, he died once for all time to conquer sin. And the life he lives, he lives for God.*

Hebrews 7:27 *He does not need to offer sacrifices every day, unlike those other high priests—first for their own sins and then for the sins of others. Jesus made one sacrifice when he offered himself. And it was sufficient for all time and all people everywhere.*

Hebrews 9:12,25-28 *His single entrance into that holy place occurred not by using the blood of goats and calves but by using his own blood—and thus obtained our redemption forever . . . 25 Nor does he repeatedly offer himself like the high priest does every year, who uses blood that is not his own. 26 Otherwise, he would have needed to suffer repeatedly since the world began. But now, during the apex of the ages, he sacrificed himself to annul sin. And he only needed to do it once for all time.*

27 Just as people are destined to die only once and then judged afterward, 28 so was Christ sacrificed just once to remove the sins of many. When he appears a second time, it will not be to deal with sin but to save those waiting for him.

Hebrews 10:10-14 *It is God's will that we are purified and made spotless through the one-time sacrifice of the body of Jesus Christ. 11 Whereas every priest under the Law of Moses performed daily rituals and repeatedly offered the same sacrifices that could never remove sins. 12 But Jesus offered one sacrifice for sins, once for all time, and now sits on the right-hand side of God. 13 He is now just waiting for the appointed time when his enemies will be placed under his feet. 14 For by one sacrifice, he has forever perfected those who are being purified and made spotless.*

1 Peter 3:18 *Because Christ suffered a single time for sins, the righteous for the unrighteous, to bring you to God. He was put to death in the body but made alive in the Spirit.*

Jesus is Human

Things to Ponder

1. *How many times will Jesus atone for the sins of humanity? What was it about him that allowed him to accomplish that task?*

2. *Is Christ's sacrifice infinite in scope and duration, or is it limited to just a few and only for a specific period? Explain your thoughts.*

3. *Is there anyone, anywhere, who is excluded from the scope of Christ's infinite Atonement?*

4. *Why was Christ's one-time Atonement sufficient for all humanity for all time? Explain.*

Chapter 4: Jesus is the Creator

Three different biblical authors (John, Paul, and the Hebraist) taught God the Father had Jesus create the universe.

This sounds ridiculous since our understanding of the universe drastically differs from those living thousands of years ago. Modern science tells us our universe is unimaginably large and incomprehensively old – the observable portion is at least 91 billion light years across and around 13.8 billion years old. It contains trillions of galaxies like our Milky Way, each having hundreds of billions of stars and trillions of planets and moons.

The cosmology of our ancestors was limited to an indefinable reality: All they knew was that they lived on land and that seas extended beyond the horizon. There was a sky where clouds and birds were seen and where rain and snow came from. There was a sun, moon, some wandering stars like Venus and Mars, and immovable stars that they could imagine formed images (constellations). That was all they knew. They had no idea how far the stars were, what those wandering objects of light were, or what made up those faint objects they could see during clear moonless nights. When describing the totality of reality, they used catch-all terms such as "all things" or "everything that can be seen and cannot be seen." God is all-powerful because he created "all things." He made everything that can be seen and cannot be seen.

This means that although their cosmology was different than ours, the central doctrines straddle *both* worldviews: God created "all things/the universe" through Jesus, and the size and age of "all things/the universe" are *irrelevant* to the subject.

The real issue is whether the claim is true or false.

4.1 Jesus Created the Universe

John 1:3,10,14 He created the universe. Nothing exists that he did not create . . . 10 He went and lived on Earth. And even though he created it, the world's inhabitants did not know who he was . . . 14 The Word became flesh and lived among us. We have seen his glory—the glory of the only Son of the Father, full of grace and truth.

Colossians 1:13-17 *He has rescued us from the subjugation of darkness and resettled us to the kingdom of his beloved Son, 14 in whom we have been redeemed and had our sins forgiven. 15 He is the image of the God who has never been seen, and existed before the universe was created. 16 He created the universe. Everything in heaven and earth, everything we see and cannot see, including thrones, powers, rulers, or authorities; he created them all, and they are for him. 17 He existed before the universe and causes it to hold together.*

Hebrews 1:8-12 *But to the Son, he said: "Your throne, O God, will last forever. You rule your kingdom with a scepter of righteousness. 9 You have loved righteousness and hated wickedness. Therefore, O God, your God, has anointed you with the oil of joy above anyone else. 10 And in the beginning, you, Lord, laid the foundation of the earth. Your hands created the heavens." 11 They will inevitably pass away, but you will always exist. They will wear out like old clothing. 12*

You will fold them up like a cloak and change them, but you will always stay the same and will live forever."

Hebrews 2:10 *It was appropriate that he who inherited the universe and created it, and who brings many children to glory as the source of their salvation, would become perfect through his suffering.*

Things to Ponder
1. Who created the universe?
2. Were the biblical writers describing just this world, or were they referring to the totality of reality, which we now understand as the universe containing trillions of galaxies?

3. *Is there anything in the universe that Jesus did not create?*

4. *Given the age and size of the universe, why would its Creator come to this planet 2000 years ago? What does that tell you about who we are and why we are so important to the Creator?*

4.2 God the Father Created the Universe Through Jesus

1 Corinthians 8:6 To us, there is only one God, the Father, the originator of the universe and for whom we live; and there is one Lord Jesus Christ, the creator of the universe and creator of humankind.

Hebrews 1:2-3 And now, God has spoken to us through his Son in these last days. God has given the universe to him as an inheritance, and created it through him. 3 The Son radiates God's glory and is the exact copy of the very essence of God. He sustains the universe by the power of his word. After he made the purification for sins, he sat down on the right-hand side of the majestic God in heaven!

Revelation 3:14 Write this in a letter to the angel of the church in Laodicea, "The Amen who is the faithful and true witness and the one who caused God's creation."

Jesus is the Creator

Things to Ponder

1. Who had Jesus create the universe?

2. If Jesus was the "Builder," the Father was the ... (Designer, Construction Manager, Owner, etc.)

3. Is a Designer or Architect the "Creator" of an object they instructed a Builder to create? Can both the Designer and Builder be the "Creator"?

4. *Both the Father and Jesus wanted Jesus to become human to conjoin the human and divine natures together and to suffer, die, and destroy death for our sakes. Why? What makes us so important to the Designer and Builder of the universe?*

Chapter 5: Jesus Upgrades Earth

One of the most overlooked aspects of Jesus in Christianity is his role in destroying this Earth and replacing it with a glorified version after he comes again.

This may seem like a waste or ultimate evil, but that is not how the Bible describes it. It is not destruction for the sake of destruction but a replacement with a better version that is superior to the original in every way. (This is not a foreign concept to anyone who designs software or produces a product for sale – a new version needs to be better than an older one.) Those who glimpsed it in revelation prayed for it to happen as soon as possible because the replacement new Earth is worth destroying the existing world.

5.1 The Earth Will Be Upgraded

> *Matthew 19:28 And Jesus said to them, "I am telling you most assuredly that when the Son of Man sits on his glorious throne at the renewal of the world, you who have followed me will sit on twelve thrones and judge the twelve tribes of Israel."*

Hebrew 1:10-12 *And in the beginning, you, Lord, laid the foundation of the earth. Your hands created the heavens." 11 They will inevitably pass away, but you will always exist. They will wear out like old clothing. 12 You will fold them up like a cloak and change them, but you will always stay the same and will live forever."*

2 Peter 3:10-13 *The day of the Lord will come unexpectedly, like a thief in the night. The sky will disappear with a terrible roar, and the Earth's materials will burn away, exposing all its secrets and evil deeds.*

11 Since these things are going to disappear, what type of person should you then be? You should be righteous and godly, 12 looking forward to the day of God, and pushing for it to come sooner, where the sky burns, and the Earth's materials melt from the heat. 13 This is so that his promise of a new heaven and new earth will finally occur, where only righteousness dwells.

Revelation 21:1,5 *And I saw a new earth and sky, for the earlier earth and sky had disappeared, and the sea disappeared as well . .*

Jesus Upgrades Earth | 131

. 5 The one sitting on the throne said, "Look! I am making everything new! Write these down for these words are trustworthy and true."

Revelation 20:11 *And I saw a great white throne and the one who sat on it. The Earth and its sky vanished from his presence and could not be found anywhere.*

Romans 8:19-21 *All of creation eagerly waits in anticipation for God to reveal who his Children are!*

20 Creation became corrupt, not through its own fault, but because God subjected it in the hope 21 that after creation is freed from its bondage to decay, it will share in the freedom of the glory of the Children of God.

Things to Ponder

1. *What will happen to the Earth, and what will replace it?*

2. Is replacing this Earth with a new version necessarily bad, or is it something "creation" itself wants?

3. Why would "creation" (the universe, this Earth, or created beings) want to be freed from "corruption" ("subject to nothingness")? What is it, or for what are they hoping?

4. *Think deeper about the implication of creation becoming free from decay (Entropy? Death? Evil?) by sharing "in the freedom of the glory of the Children of God." What does that look like? Could Christ's control over the forces of the universe have anything to do with this change? Explain.*

Chapter 6: Jesus is the Savior

One of the most common themes in the New Testament is that Jesus is our Savior. This is said in many ways: He is our Redeemer; he paid the ransom that the law demanded because we sinned; he suffered and died as a sacrificial substitute for us; he removed our sins; he reconciles us to God; he intercedes and mediates on our behalf to the Father; and more.

This chapter looks at different aspects of Jesus Christ being our Savior. There are nuances in the differences that are worth exploring.

6.1 Jesus Paid the Ransom for Humanity's Sins

Matthew 20:28 Just as the Son of Man did not come to Earth to be served, but to serve and give his life as a ransom for many.

Galatians 1:4 He surrendered himself for our sins so that he may ransom us from the current wicked age, following the will of our God and Father.

Galatians 3:13 Christ paid our ransom from the curse of the law and became a curse for us, for it is written, "Those who hang on a tree are cursed."

1 Timothy 2:6 *He gave himself as a ransom for all, and is witnessed to all the world at the right time.*

Titus 2:14 *He gave himself for us so he could pay our ransom from all wickedness and purify for himself a special elite who are eager to do good works.*

1 Peter 1:18-20 *As you know, gold and silver were not used to pay your ransom from the futile life you received from your ancestors, 19 but with the incalculably valuable blood of Christ, the unblemished and spotless Lamb of God, 20 who was chosen before the world was created, and was revealed in these last days for your sake.*

Revelation 1:5 *And from Jesus Christ, who is the faithful witness, the first to resurrect from the dead, and the ruler of all kings of the earth. Praise him who loves us and who used his blood to ransom us from our sins!*

Jesus is the Savior | 137

Things to Ponder

1. *What did Jesus do to liberate us from the consequences of our sins?*

2. *Jesus paid our ransom from what? What would happen to us if he did not pay the ransom?*

3. *Think of an example of someone held for ransom. Can they be voluntarily freed without an exchanged payment?*

4. *Think deeply: Why was Christ's life or "blood" an acceptable exchange to liberate all of us? Why would "Justice" (the punishment for sin) accept Christ's payment of himself as an acceptable exchange for all of us?*

6.2 Jesus Suffered and Died as Our Sacrifice

John 17:19 I sanctify myself for their sakes so that they also might be sanctified by the truth.

Romans 3:23-25 All of us are sinners and fall short of God's glory, 24 but now are justified for free by his grace, through the redemption that is in Christ Jesus, 25 – whom God presented as an appeasement through faith in his blood. God's righteousness shows because he restrained himself from punishing previously committed sins.

Romans 8:32 Since God did not spare his own Son but gave him up for our sakes, there is then nothing that he would not also give us.

Hebrews 10:10-20 It is God's will that we are purified and made spotless through the one-time sacrifice of the body of Jesus Christ.

11 Whereas every priest under the Law of Moses performed daily rituals and repeatedly offered the same sacrifices that could never remove sins. 12 But Jesus offered one sacrifice for sins, once for all time, and now sits on the right-hand side of God. 13 He is now just waiting for the appointed time when his enemies will be placed under his feet. 14 For by one sacrifice, he has forever perfected those who are being purified and made spotless.

15 The Holy Spirit also witnesses to us about this, for he says, 16 "'This is the covenant I will make with them after those days,' says the Lord. 'I will put my laws into their hearts and write them on their minds.'" 17 [He then adds] "I will never remember their sins and lawless acts anymore." 18 After sins are forgiven, sacrifice for sin is no longer needed.

19 And so, my brothers and sisters, because of the blood of Jesus, we can confidently enter the holiest place in heaven, 20 using a new way to enter — his flesh pushes the barrier open for us.

1 Peter 1:11,18-20 *They sought to know the time and circumstance the Spirit of Christ was alluding to when he told them in advance that the Messiah would suffer, and the great glory afterward . . . 18 As you know, gold and silver were not used to pay your ransom from the futile life you received from your ancestors, 19 but with the incalculably valuable blood of Christ, the unblemished and spotless Lamb of God, 20 who was chosen before the world was* *created, and was revealed in these last days for your sake.*

1 Peter 2:21-24 *You were called for this purpose because Christ suffered for you. He is your example; follow his footsteps. 22 He never sinned and never deceived anyone. 23 When they vilified him, he did not retaliate. When he suffered, he did not make threats. He just relied upon God, who always judges justly. 24 He bore our sins in his body on the cross so that we would die to sin but then live for righteousness. His wounds have healed you!*

1 John 4:9-10,14 *God showed his love toward us by sending his only Son into the world so that we might live through him. 10 This is real love: Not that we loved God, but because He loved us — and sent his Son to be the appeasing sacrifice for our sins! . . . 14 And we have seen and testify that the Father sent his Son to be the Savior of humankind.*

Things to Ponder

1. *Did Jesus suffer for us? Provide several reasons why he did what he did for us.*

2. *What did his sacrifice do? Why was it necessary?*

Jesus is the Savior | 143

3. *How often must the sacrifice occur to cover all humanity for all time? Explain.*

4. <u>*When*</u> *was Christ chosen to become our sacrifice? What does that tell you about God's foreknowledge and responsibility concerning Adam and Eve?*

> 5. Think deeper. What was Jesus Christ's <u>value</u> that made his one-time Atonement sufficient to save all humans for all time? Share your thoughts on what he did.

6.3 Jesus Died for Humanity

John 10:15,17-18 As the Father knows me, I also know the Father. I lay down my life for the sheep . . . 17 The Father loves me because I willingly lay down my life so that I might take it back. 18 No one takes it from me—I voluntarily lay it down. I have the authority to let myself die and the authority to come back to life. My Father ordered me to do this.

Romans 5:6-8 *For while we were powerless, Christ died at the appointed time for us sinners. 7 It is rare for someone to give up his life for a righteous person except, perhaps, for an especially good man. 8 But God proved his great love for us—although we were sinners, Christ died for us!*

2 Corinthians 5:14-15 *Christ's love controls us because we are convinced that he died for all; thus, all died. 15 He died for all so that those who live will no longer live for themselves, but for the one who died and rose again.*

Galatians 2:20-21 *I have been crucified with Christ. I no longer live—Christ is the one who lives in me. I live the life I now have in this earthly body by having faith in the Son of God—who loved me and gave himself up for me. 21 I do not cast aside the grace of God since if obedience to the Law could make us righteous, then Christ died for nothing.*

1 Thessalonians 5:9-10 *God did not destine us for condemnation but to obtain salvation through our Lord, Jesus Christ, 10 who died for us. Whether we are still alive or already dead when he returns, we will live with him!*

Hebrews 2:9-10 *Jesus was temporarily made lower than angels. He is now crowned with glory and honor because he subjected himself to death. By God's grace, he died for everyone! 10 It was appropriate that he who inherited the universe and created it, and who brings many children to glory as the source of their salvation, would become perfect through his suffering.*

Hebrews 9:15,26-28 *This is why he mediates the new covenant so that those called will receive an eternal inheritance—because his death ransomed them from the punishments they deserved for transgressions done under the first covenant . . . 26 Otherwise, he would have needed to suffer repeatedly since the world began. But now, during the apex of the ages, he sacrificed himself to annul sin. And he only needed to do it once for all time.*

27 Just as people are destined to die only once and then judged afterward, 28 so was Christ sacrificed just once to remove the sins of many. When he appears a second time, it will not be to deal with sin but to save those waiting for him.

Jesus is the Savior | 147

Things to Ponder
1. *For whom did Jesus die?*
2. *Did Jesus die willingly or unwillingly?*

3. What did Jesus receive for his willingness to die for us?

4. What did his death do? Give several results.

5. Think deeper: Why did his sacrifice work?

6. Think deeper again: When and how did Jesus become perfect? Is perfection and being "God" the same thing? Explain.

6.4 Jesus Christ's Sacrifice/Blood Reconciles Us to God

Romans 5:9-11 Since his blood has now justified us, he will have saved us from God's wrath. 10 For if we were reconciled to God through the death of his Son while we were still his enemies, how much more shall his resurrection save us? 11 Furthermore, we are also rejoicing in God through our Lord Jesus Christ, by whom we have received reconciliation.

Ephesians 2:13-16 But now, in Christ Jesus, you who were once far away are brought near by the blood of Christ. 14 For he is our peace, and have made both Jews and Gentiles into one people, and broke down the wall of hostility that separated us. 15 In his flesh, he annulled the Law's commandments in its decrees, to make peace between the Jew and Gentile, and create one new people, 16 so that he might reconcile both groups as one people to God using the cross, which destroys the hostility between both groups.

Colossians 1:20-22 And through Jesus, God reconciled the universe to himself, whether things on earth or in the heavens—by making peace through Jesus's blood on the cross. 21 You were once alienated from God, with a hostile mind because of your evil actions. 22 But now, Jesus has reconciled you in his flesh through his death, to present you to God, holy, unblemished, and beyond reproach.

Hebrews 7:25-28 *Consequently, he can utterly save those who come to God through him since he is always there to intercede for them. 26 He is the high priest we need, one who is holy, innocent, pure—and distinct from us sinners. He has been exalted above the heavens. 27 He does not need to offer sacrifices every day, unlike those other high priests—first for their own sins and then for the sins of others. Jesus made one sacrifice when he offered himself. And it was sufficient for all time and all people everywhere. 28 The law appoints men to become high priests who had weaknesses, but God's oath, which was given after the law, appointed the Son, who is now perfected once and for all.*

Hebrews 9:11-28 *But Christ came as the high priest of the good things that are to come. He* *entered into the greater and more perfect tabernacle, which is not made by human hands or of this world.*

12 His single entrance into that holy place occurred not by using the blood of goats and calves but by using his own blood—and thus obtained our redemption forever.

13 If the blood of goats and bulls and the ashes of a young cow that are sprinkled on those who are unclean can cleanse people's bodies, 14 how much more the blood of Christ, who offered himself unblemished to God through the eternal Spirit, shall purify our consciousness from dead works so that we may serve the living God! 15 This is why he mediates the new covenant so that those called will receive an eternal inheritance—because his death ransomed them from the punishments they deserved for transgressions done under the first covenant.

16 For when there is a will, it is necessary to verify that the owner of the will is actually dead, 17 because a will can only be enforced after the owner is deceased. It cannot take effect as long as the owner is still alive. 18 This is why the first covenant needed blood to become effective. 19 After Moses told the people every one of the commandments, he mixed the blood of calves and goats with water and, using a branch of a hyssop tree and some scarlet-colored wool, sprinkled the scroll and the assembled people, 20 saying, "This is the blood of the covenant that God commanded you to follow." 21 Moses also sprinkled with blood the tabernacle and all the objects used in the worship ceremony. 22 In fact, the Law requires blood to purify almost all things. There can be no forgiveness without the shedding of blood. 23 It was then necessary for the poor imitations of heavenly things to be purified in this manner. But the heavenly versions require better sacrifices than merely using the blood of animals.

24 For Christ did not enter into the tabernacle made by human hands (which is just a poor copy of the true one), he entered into heaven itself to appear before God's presence on our behalf. 25 Nor does he repeatedly offer himself like the high priest does every year, who uses blood that is not his own. 26 Otherwise, he

would have needed to suffer repeatedly since the world began. But now, during the apex of the ages, he sacrificed himself to annul sin. And he only needed to do it once for all time. 27 Just as people are destined to die only once and then judged afterward, 28 so was Christ sacrificed just once to remove the sins of many. When he appears a second time, it will not be to deal with sin but to save those waiting for him.

1 Peter 3:18 *Because Christ suffered a single time for sins, the righteous for the unrighteous, to bring you to God. He was put to death in the body but made alive in the Spirit.*

Revelation 1:5 *And from Jesus Christ, who is the faithful witness, the first to resurrect from the dead, and the ruler of all kings of the earth. Praise him who loves us and who used his blood to ransom us from our sins!*

Revelation 5:9 *And they sang a new song, saying, "You are worthy to take the scroll and break its seals. For you were slaughtered and used your blood to purchase people unto God out of every tribe, language, ethnicity, and nation."*

Jesus is the Savior | 155

Things to Ponder

1. *What effect did Christ's sacrifice do on our relationship with God the Father?*

2. *What did his sacrifice do for religious and ethnic relations?*

3. What does Christ's sacrifice do _to_ us when we are brought into God's presence?

4. How often must Christ perform his sacrifice? Why?

Jesus is the Savior | 157

5. *What needed to be shed for us to be forgiven? Why?*

6. *Think deeper: How extensive was the reconciliation that came from Christ's sacrifice? Was it only between humans and God? Explain.*

6.5 Jesus Christ's Blood Forgives Sins

Matthew 26:28 This is indeed my blood of the covenant; it is poured out to forgive the sins of many people.

Luke 22:15-16,19-20 Jesus said, "I've been looking forward to eating this Passover meal with you before I suffer. 16 I won't eat this meal again until it is fulfilled in the kingdom of God." . . . 19 He took some bread and gave thanks to God for it. He broke it into pieces, and gave it to them saying, "This is my body, which is given for you. Do this to remember me." 20 After eating, he took the cup of wine and said, "This cup is the new covenant of my blood, which is poured out for you."

Luke 22:42-44 Jesus said, "Father, if you are willing, please take this cup away from me. Nonetheless, let your will be done, not mine."

43 An angel then appeared from heaven and encouraged him to go through with it. 44 While being subjected to incomprehensible agony, he prayed to the Father even more fervently, and his sweat looked like blood and fell to the ground in clumps.

Ephesians 1:7 *In whom we have been redeemed through his blood and had our sins forgiven due to his rich grace.*

Hebrews 9:11-14 *But Christ came as the high priest of the good things that are to come. He entered into the greater and more perfect tabernacle, which is not made by human hands or of this world. 12 His single entrance into that holy place occurred not by using the blood of goats and calves but by using his own blood—and thus obtained our redemption forever.*

13 If the blood of goats and bulls and the ashes of a young cow that are sprinkled on those who are unclean can cleanse people's bodies, 14 how much more the blood of Christ, who offered himself unblemished to God through the eternal Spirit, shall purify our consciousness from dead works so that we may serve the living God!

1 John 1:7 *But if we walk in the light, as he is in the light, we participate with one another, and the blood of his Son, Jesus, cleanses us from all sin.*

Things to Ponder
1. What did Christ's shed blood do?
2. Was Jesus looking forward to his sacrifice? What were the emotions he was feeling immediately before his sacrifice?

3. What did Jesus feel when he sacrificed himself?

4. How should you feel toward Christ for what he went through for you? Express yourself.

> 5. *Think deeper: Why did Jesus use bread and wine to represent his body and blood? What does eating it do for us?*

6.6 Jesus Annuls Sin

***Hebrews 9:26** Otherwise, he would have needed to suffer repeatedly since the world began. But now, during the apex of the ages, he sacrificed himself to annul sin. And he only needed to do it once for all time.*

Jesus is the Savior | 163

Things to Ponder

1. What did Jesus do to sin?

2. What does it mean to "annul" something?

3. How many times did Jesus need to annul sin?

4. *Think deeper: The annulment of sin was done between Jesus and "Justice," where Jesus paid the price of all of humanity's sins for all time. Those who follow him avoid Justice's punishment, while those who refuse are exposed.*

   Does the annulment of sin mean we can do all the evil we want without consequence? Explain.

6.7 Jesus Christ's Grace Saves Us

***Romans 5:19-21** For as one man's disobedience resulted in many becoming sinners, so many will become righteous because of one man's obedience. 20 The coming of the Law boosted the transgression; but where sin increased, grace increased even more, 21 so that as sin reigned in death, so also grace might reign in righteousness, giving eternal life through our Lord Jesus Christ.*

***Ephesians 1:7** In whom we have been redeemed through his blood and had our sins forgiven due to his rich grace.*

Things to Ponder
1. *Is Christ's "grace" or charity more than capable of saving us?*

2. *Is a "crime" committed if there is no law that says a specific action is illegal?*

3. *Did Christ's grace outpace the effects of sin? What do you think this means?*

4. *What is the final reward of the righteous? Explain.*

6.8 Jesus Condemned Sin Through His Flesh

Romans 8:3 *God did what the Law of Moses was incapable of doing due to the weakness of flesh: God condemned sin in the flesh by sending his own Son to become flesh.*

1 Peter 2:24 *He bore our sins in his body on the cross so that we would die to sin but then live for righteousness. His wounds have healed you!*

1 Peter 3:18 *Because Christ suffered a single time for sins, the righteous for the unrighteous,* *to bring you to God. He was put to death in the body but made alive in the Spirit.*

Things to Ponder
1. How did God condemn sin?
2. Who took upon himself the consequences of our sins? How?

Jesus is the Savior | 169

3. What healed us? When and how?

4. How often will Christ suffer for us? Explain.

6.9 Jesus Saves Us From Our Sins

Matthew 1:21 She will give birth to a son, and you will name him "Jesus" because he will save his people from their sins.

2 Corinthians 5:18-21 All of this is from God, who reconciled us to himself through Christ, and who gave us the ministry of reconciliation.

19 God was in Christ and was reconciling the world to himself by not holding humanity's sins against them. He has given us the message of reconciliation. 20 As a result, we are Christ's ambassadors. God is pleading with you through us: "Be reconciled to God!" 21 For he had made the sinless Christ become a sin for us, so that we may become the righteousness of God through him.

Revelation 1:5 And from Jesus Christ, who is the faithful witness, the first to resurrect from the dead, and the ruler of all kings of the earth. Praise him who loves us and who used his blood to ransom us from our sins!

Galatians 1:4 He surrendered himself for our sins so that he may ransom us from the current *wicked age, following the will of our God and Father.*

Titus 2:14 *He gave himself for us so he could pay our ransom from all wickedness and purify for himself a special elite who are eager to do good works.*

1 Peter 2:21-24 *You were called for this purpose because Christ suffered for you. He is your example; follow his footsteps. 22 He never sinned and never deceived anyone. 23 When they vilified him, he did not retaliate. When he suffered, he did not make threats. He just relied upon God, who always judges justly. 24 He bore our sins in his body on the cross so that we would die to sin but then live for righteousness. His wounds have healed you!*

1 John 2:1-2 *My children, I am writing these things to you so that you will not sin. But if anyone does sin, we have an advocate on our behalf with the Father—Jesus Christ, the righteous. 2 He is the sacrifice that pays for our sins, not just for our sins, but for the sins of all humankind.*

172 | This is Jesus Christ

Revelation 1:5 *And from Jesus Christ, who is the faithful witness, the first to resurrect from the dead, and the ruler of all kings of the earth. Praise him who loves us and who used his blood to ransom us from our sins!*

Things to Ponder
1. What did Christ save us from?
2. Why did Christ save us? What was God's goal?

Jesus is the Savior | 173

3. What did Christ use to save us?

4. What does God expect from those whose sins are forgiven?

6.10 Jesus Takes Away Our Sins

John 1:29 The next day, John sees Jesus coming toward him and proclaims, "Look! The Lamb of God, who takes away the sins of humankind!"

1 John 1:7 But if we walk in the light, as he is in the light, we participate with one another, and the blood of his Son, Jesus, cleanses us from all sin.

1 John 3:5,8-9 You know that Jesus came to remove sins—and there is no sin in him . . . 8 The devil owns those who sin because he has been sinning from the beginning. This is why the Son of God came—to destroy the devil's work. 9 Those born of God do not sin because God's seed is growing in them; they cannot go on sinning because they are God's children.

Jesus is the Savior | 175

Things to Ponder

1. What did Jesus do to our sins?

2. What are we after our sins are taken away?

3. Who owns those who sin?

4. Think deeper: What does "Those born of God do not commit sin" mean? Is it a license to do whatever we want and ignore God's command for us to obey him?

6.11 Those Who Believe in Jesus Get Their Sins Forgiven

Mark 16:16 Whoever believes and gets baptized will be saved, but whoever refuses to believe will be condemned.

Acts 10:43 All the prophets testified of him, whereby everyone who believes in him will have their sins forgiven through his name.

Acts 13:37-39 But he whom God raised from the dead did not experience decomposition. 38 My friends, you should know that through this man is proclaimed the forgiveness of sins. 39 Through him, all who believe are set free from all their sins—something the Law of Moses could never do.

Things to Ponder

1. What is needed for salvation?

2. Why did Jesus add baptism to the condition for salvation? What does this tell you about the need for behavior for true belief? Explain.

Jesus is the Savior | 179

3. What did Christ do to our sins?

4. Can we be "saved" without belief in Christ and baptism? Explain.

6.12 Consuming Christ's "Flesh" and "Blood" Saves Us

John 6:32-69 Jesus told them, "I am telling you truthfully, Moses did not give you the bread from heaven. Rather, my Father gives you the true bread from heaven. 33 For the bread of God is the bread who comes down from heaven and gives life to the world."

34 They then said, "Lord, always give us this bread!"

35 Jesus then said, "I am the bread of life. Whoever comes to me will never hunger, and whoever believes in me will never thirst. 36 But I tell you, you have seen me but still do not believe me. 37 All those the Father gave me will come to me, and I will never reject them. 38 God sent me down from heaven to do what he wants, not what I want. 39 When he sent me to earth, he wanted me to keep all those he gave me and elevate them on the last day. 40 He who sent me wants everyone who looks to the Son and believes in him to have eternal life—and I will elevate them on the last day."

41 The Jews started to grumble because he said he was the living bread that came down from heaven. 42 They then said, "Isn't this Jesus, Joseph's son? We know his parents! How can he now claim to have come down from heaven?"

43 Jesus told them, "Stop grumbling! 44 No one can come unto me unless the one who sent me, the Father, pulls him. I will then elevate him on the last day. 45 As it is written in the Prophets, 'God shall teach them all.' Everyone who listens to the Father and learns from him comes to me. 46 No one has seen the Father, except the one who came from God—he has seen him. 47 I am telling you truthfully, he who believes has eternal life. I am the bread of life. 49 Your ancestors ate manna in the wilderness and died. 50 All who eat this bread from heaven will never die. 51 I am the living bread that came down from heaven. Whoever eats this bread will live forever. The bread that I give for the life of humanity is my flesh."

52 The Jews started to dispute among themselves, saying, "How can this man give us his flesh to eat?"

53 Then Jesus said to them, "I am telling you the truth—unless you eat the flesh of the Son

of Man and drink his blood, you will not have real 'Life' within you. 54 Whoever eats my flesh and drinks my blood has eternal life, and I will elevate that person on the last day. 55 For my flesh is 'True Food,' and my blood is 'True Drink.' 56 Whoever eats my flesh and drinks my blood lives within me and I in them. 57 I live because of the Father, who sent me. Those who eat my flesh will live because of me. 58 This is the bread from heaven. Unlike your ancestors who ate manna and died, whoever eats this bread will live forever."

59 (He said these things while teaching in the synagogue in Capernaum.)

60 When they heard this, many of his disciples said, "This is hard to accept; who can tolerate hearing it?"

61 Jesus knew that his disciples were grumbling about what he was saying, so he asked them, "Do my words offend you? 62 What if you were to see the Son of Man ascend to where he was before? 63 The Spirit is the one who gives life; not the flesh, which is useless. The words I told you are spirit and are life itself. 64 But there are some of you who do not believe." For Jesus knew from the beginning who did not believe and who would betray him. 65 Then Jesus said, "This is why I told you that no one can come unto me unless the Father allows it."

66 After hearing this, many of his disciples stopped following him.

67 Then Jesus said to the twelve, "Do you also wish to leave?"

68 Simon Peter answered, "Lord, to whom shall we go? You have the words of eternal life. 69 And we believe and are certain that you are the Messiah, the Son of the living God!"

Things to Ponder
1. What is the bread?

184 | This is Jesus Christ

2. *Think deeper: What happens to us when we eat the bread?*

3. *Where did the bread come from? Why?*

Jesus is the Savior | 185

4. *Important! Is it critical to eat Christ's "flesh" and drink his "blood"? Can we mutually indwell with him and receive eternal life without doing so? Explain.*

5. *Think deeper: Why was it so hard for people to accept what Jesus said? What was so offensive that most left him? Also, if Jesus were talking symbolically, why didn't he say so since it would have prevented his disciples from leaving him?*

6.13 Jesus Reconciles Man to God

Romans 5:10-11 *For if we were reconciled to God through the death of his Son while we were still his enemies, how much more shall his resurrection save us? 11 Furthermore, we are also rejoicing in God through our Lord Jesus Christ, by whom we have received reconciliation.*

2 Corinthians 5:18-21 *All of this is from God, who reconciled us to himself through Christ, and who gave us the ministry of reconciliation. 19 God was in Christ and was reconciling the world to himself by not holding humanity's sins against them. He has given us the message of reconciliation.*

20 As a result, we are Christ's ambassadors. God is pleading with you through us: "Be reconciled to God!" 21 For he had made the sinless Christ become a sin for us, so that we may become the righteousness of God through him.

Ephesians 2:16 *So that he might reconcile both groups as one people to God using the* *cross, which destroys the hostility between both groups.*

Colossians 1:20-22 *And through Jesus, God reconciled the universe to himself, whether things on earth or in the heavens—by making peace through Jesus's blood on the cross.*

21 You were once alienated from God, with a hostile mind because of your evil actions. 22 But now, Jesus has reconciled you in his flesh through his death, to present you to God, holy, unblemished, and beyond reproach.

Things to Ponder
1. *What did Christ's sacrifice do for our relationship with the Father?*

Jesus is the Savior | 189

2. *How can we become "the righteousness of God"?*

3. *Think deeper: What happens to us after we are reconciled with God?*

> 4. *Think deeper again: Are humans the only things Christ's death reconciled with God? What else? What does that tell you about reality?*

6.14 Jesus Intercedes/Mediates on Behalf of Man to God

> **Romans 8:34** *Who can condemn? Christ Jesus is the one who died, who rose again, and who is even now on the right-hand side of God interceding for us.*

1 Timothy 2:5 There is one God and one mediator between God and men: The man Jesus Christ!

Hebrews 7:25 Consequently, he can utterly save those who come to God through him since he is always there to intercede for them.

Hebrews 8:6 But now, Jesus's ministry is vastly better – just as the covenant he mediates is also vastly better – and enacted on better promises.

Hebrews 9:15,24 This is why he mediates the new covenant so that those called will receive an eternal inheritance—because his death ransomed them from the punishments they deserved for transgressions done under the first covenant . . . 24 For Christ did not enter into the tabernacle made by human hands (which is just a poor copy of the true one), he entered into heaven itself to appear before God's presence on our behalf.

Hebrews 12:24 And to Jesus, the mediator of the new covenant, and to the sprinkling of blood, which speaks of better things than the blood of Abel.

1 John 2:1 *My children, I am writing these things to you so that you will not sin. But if anyone does sin, we have an advocate on our behalf with the Father—Jesus Christ, the righteous.*

Things to Ponder
1. What is Jesus doing on our behalf?
2. How many mediators are there between God and us?

Jesus is the Savior | 193

3. *What do we receive by Christ's mediation?*

4. *Think deeper: Why would Christ go through the trouble? What could his motivation be for mediating? What does he get out of it?*

Chapter 7: Jesus Conquered Death

The most incredible story in the Bible is the repeated claim that Jesus came back to life after being dead for three days. He then interacted with his followers for over a month before physically rising into the sky and returning to God.

Jesus had the power within himself to subject himself to death and the power to conquer it. His resurrection is the completion of his infinite Atonement and is proof to all that he succeeded in accomplishing his goal. **There is now *no* risk of failure**, and it is only a matter of time before he returns to usher in the next stage of our evolution and the final fate of all.

This is not all. The Bible also emphasizes that Christ's resurrection was not to prove that he was who he asserted to be, but was done to destroy death itself, so that all humans will enjoy a gift, regardless of their righteousness: <u>Immortality</u>. This is where everyone will eventually receive immortal physical bodies at some point in the future, and will not remain disembodied spirits forever.

This chapter examines different aspects of his resurrection.

7.1 Jesus Rose From the Dead

John 10:17-18 The Father loves me because I willingly lay down my life so that I might take it back. 18 No one takes it from me—I voluntarily lay it down. I have the authority to let myself die and the authority to come back to life. My Father ordered me to do this.

Matthew 28:5-9 The angel said to the women, "Do not be afraid! I know you are looking for Jesus, who was crucified. 6 He is not here—he has risen from the dead—just as he promised! Come! See where his body laid. 7 Hurry and tell his disciples he has risen from the dead and has gone ahead of them into Galilee, where they will be able to see him. Do not forget to tell them this message!"

8 As they hastily left the tomb with fear and great joy, and were rushing to tell the disciples what the angel instructed, 9 Jesus met them and said, "Greetings!" They then prostrated themselves before him and held on to his feet, and worshiped him.

Jesus Conquered Death

Luke 24:36-51 While they were talking about these things, Jesus suddenly appeared in their midst and said, "May you have peace." 37 They then jumped in terror and feared they saw a ghost. 38 He said to them, "Why are you frightened? Why are your hearts filled with doubt? 39 Look at my hands and my feet. It is me! Touch me and confirm it is me. A ghost does not have a body of flesh and bone that you see I have."

40 He then showed them his hands and feet. 41 And while they still couldn't believe it was him out of sheer joy and amazement, he asked them, "Do you have anything to eat?" 42 They then handed him some broiled fish, 43 which he then ate in front of them.

44 He then said, "This is what I told you before—everything about me that is written in the law of Moses, the prophets, and psalms need to be fulfilled." 45 He then opened their minds so that they could completely understand the scriptures, 46 and told them, "This is what was written: 'The Messiah needs to suffer and rise from the dead after three days. 47 Repentance and forgiveness of sins are proclaimed in his name, starting in Jerusalem.' 48 You are witnesses of these things. 49 And now, I am going to send to you what my Father has promised. So, stay in the city until the power from heaven clothes you."

50 He led them close to Bethany when he then raised his hands toward heaven and blessed them. 51 While he was blessing them, he started rising up into the air and was then carried off into heaven.

Acts 1:1-11 *Theophilus, my earlier book contained everything that Jesus began to do and teach, 2 up to the day he was taken up into heaven, after giving instructions to the apostles through the Holy Spirit.*

3 For forty days after he died, he interacted with them and proved in so many ways that he was truly real and alive once more. He spoke to them of things concerning the kingdom of God.

4 And when they assembled, he told them: "Do not leave Jerusalem, but wait for the Father's promise, that I have mentioned. 5 For John baptized with water, but in just a few days, you are going to be baptized with the Holy Spirit."

6 They gathered around him and asked, "Lord, are you going to restore the kingdom of Israel at this time?" 7 He replied, "You do not need to know the time and date that the Father set. 8 But you will receive power when the Holy Spirit comes on you. You will be my witnesses in both Jerusalem and Samaria and to all the earth."

9 After he had said these things, and while they were looking at him, he started floating up into the sky until he rose so high that a cloud hid him from their sight. 10 As they looked intently toward the sky, two men in white robes suddenly appeared beside them. 11 They said, "Men of Galilee, why are you standing here staring into the sky? This same Jesus that you saw go up into the sky will return in the same manner he left."

Acts 10:40-41 *God raised him from the dead on the third day and made him appear openly. 41 Not to everyone, but to a group of witnesses who have been selected beforehand by God. That is, to us, who ate and drank with him after he rose from the dead.*

Romans 6:9-10 *Know that Christ was resurrected from the dead—he can never experience death again! Death can never again have power over him. 10 When he died, he died once for all time to conquer sin. And the life he lives, he lives for God.*

Revelation 1:18 *I am the living one. I was dead but look at me now—I am alive and will be for all eternity. I hold the keys of Death and Hades.*

Things to Ponder
1. *Did Jesus Christ come back to life?*

Jesus Conquered Death | 201

2. *Did his disciples consider the resurrected Jesus to be real or just a figment of their imagination?*

3. *Did the resurrected Jesus have a physical body comprised of matter that could be felt, could eat, and could be interacted with? What does this tell you about resurrected bodies?*

4. *How long did the resurrected Jesus interact with his disciples?*

5. *How did Jesus leave them? Will he return in the same manner? Explain.*

7.2 His Resurrection Saves Us From Death and Resurrects Us

John 5:28-29 Do not be so surprised, because the time is coming when all those who are dead will hear his voice, 29 and will come out of the grave. Those who have lived righteously will receive a resurrection of life, while those who have been evil will receive a resurrection where they will be condemned.

Acts 24:15 I have the same hope in God that these men have—that there will be a resurrection of both the righteous and unrighteous.

1 Corinthians 15:12-30 If it is being preached that Christ rose from the dead, how is it possible some of you are claiming there is no such thing as the resurrection of the dead? 13 But if there is no resurrection of the dead, then Christ did not rise from the dead either. 14 And if Christ did not rise, then our preaching is pointless, and your faith is pointless as well. 15 Not just that, but we would also be exposed as liars because we had testified that God raised up Christ when, in fact, he did not—if the dead are not resurrected. 16 For if the dead are not resurrected, neither has Christ been resurrected. 17 And if Christ has not been raised from the dead, then your faith is pointless, and you are still in your sins. 18 Furthermore, those who have already died while having faith in Christ are irretrievably gone. 19 If only in this life can we have hope in Christ, we are pitiful.

20 In reality, Christ truly rose from the dead and was the very first person to ever come back to life after dying. 21 Since death came because of a man, it is necessary for the resurrection of the dead to also come from a man.

22 In Adam, everyone dies; in Christ, everyone will live again.

23 But each according to their place in line: Christ is the first to live again, followed by those who belong to him when he returns. 24 Then the end will come when he hands over the kingdom to God the Father (after he annuls all rulers, authorities, and powers). 25 He must reign until he puts all his enemies under his feet. 26 The last enemy he will annul is death.

27 For he has dominion over all things. However, when it says, "All things," it is evident that that excludes God, who gave Jesus dominion over the universe. 28 After all things are put under the Son's authority, he then is placed under the Father's authority so that God may have dominion over all.

29 Finally, if there is no resurrection, why are those who are baptized for the dead doing it? If the dead are not going to rise, why then are they baptized for them? 30 And why are we in constant danger from others?

2 Timothy 1:10 *This plan is now shown to us by the manifestation of our Savior Jesus Christ, who destroyed death, and brought life and immortality through the gospel.*

1 John 3:2 *Dear friends, we are already the Children of God, but he has not yet revealed to us what exactly we will be, only that when Jesus appears, we will become like him, for we will see him as he truly is.*

Revelation 1:18 *I am the living one. I was dead but look at me now—I am alive and will* *be for all eternity. I hold the keys of Death and Hades.*

Things to Ponder
1. What will happen to us in the future?
2. Do both the good and bad get resurrected?

3. What happens to us after we resurrect?

4. What does "annulment" mean? If death is the separation of the spirit from the body (James 2:26), what does the annulment of death mean? Can immortal entities ever die again?

5. *Think deeper: Since Christ's resurrection was physical – his resurrected body was the reanimation of his corpse into an immortal form comprised of matter that could be felt – what would your resurrected body be like if you are transformed into becoming like him? Describe.*

> 6. *Think deeper still: What are the implications of Christ annulling death? For us, and perhaps, other life forms?*

7.3 Jesus Annulled the Devil and Controls Death and Access to the Afterlife

Hebrews 2:14-17 Since God's children are humans with flesh and blood, he, too, shared in that same nature so that by his death, he may annul the devil, who holds the power of death,

15 and liberate those who were in slavery and terrified of death.

16 He did not come to help the angels; he came to help Abraham's descendants. 17 This is why he needed to fully have the exact human nature as his siblings, so that he may be a merciful and empathetic high priest before God, and offer an authentic sacrifice for the sins of humankind.

Revelation 1:18 *I am the living one. I was dead but look at me now—I am alive and will be for all eternity. I hold the keys of Death and Hades.*

Things to Ponder
1. What did Jesus annul by his death?

Jesus Conquered Death | 211

2. Why was Christ's sacrifice "authentic"? In other words, why did it apply to humans?

3. Who controls death and access to the afterlife? Why?

4. *Think deeper: Why is it preferable to live forever with a perfected physical body than to remain a disembodied spirit? Think of all the things you can do with a physical body that you cannot do without one.*

7.4 The Resurrected Jesus is Lord of Both the Living and the Dead

Romans 14:9 *Christ died and lived again to become Lord of both the living and the dead.*

Jesus Conquered Death | 213

2 Corinthians 5:15 *He died for all so that those who live will no longer live for themselves, but for the one who died and rose again.*

Things to Ponder
1. Who is the Lord of the living and the dead?
2. What do you think it means to say someone is "Lord of both the living and the dead"?

3. *How extensive was the scope of Christ's sacrifice? Is there anyone that it did not cover?*

4. *How are we supposed to live, knowing what he did for us?*

7.5 Jesus Destroys Death and Hades (the Afterlife)

1 Corinthians 15:26 The last enemy he will annul is death.

2 Timothy 1:10 This plan is now shown to us by the manifestation of our Savior Jesus Christ, who destroyed death, and brought life and immortality through the gospel.

Revelation 20:13-14 The sea gave up the dead who were in it, and Death and Hades gave up the dead that were in them—and each person was judged according to what they did.

14 Then Death and Hades were thrown into the lake of fire. The second death is the lake of fire.

Things to Ponder
1. What is the last "enemy" Christ annuls?

2. What did Jesus bring for us?

3. Think deeper: Why would God destroy death and Hades (where we go when we die)? What does that tell you about our coming physical immortality?

Chapter 8: Jesus is the Only Way

Jesus and the biblical writers said something incredibly unpopular to other faiths or those who prefer to get along with everyone, by claiming there are many ways to heaven.

But the words were said, and their meaning will never change. We can either believe Christ or not, but we will know his words are true when we stand before him for judgment.

8.1 No One Can be Saved or Approach God Without Going Through Jesus

John 14:6 Jesus said to them, "I am the Way, and the Truth, and the Life. No one can come unto the Father except through me."

Acts 4:10-12 Know this, you people of Israel, that this man was healed due to the name of Jesus Christ of Nazareth, whom you crucified, but whom God raised from the dead. 11 Jesus is the stone that the builders rejected that is now the cornerstone. 12 Salvation cannot be found in anyone else! There is no other name given to humankind that can save us!

***1 Timothy* 2:5** *There is one God and one mediator between God and men: The man Jesus Christ!*

***Revelation* 7:17** *Because the Lamb, who is right before the throne of God, will be their shepherd and lead them to springs of living water. God will wipe away every tear from their eyes.*

Things to Ponder
1. Can anyone approach the Father without going through Jesus Christ?
2. Who is the gatekeeper who stands between all humans and God?

Jesus is the Only Way | 219

3. Who is the one mediator between God and humans?

4. Is there any other name that can save us?

5. Thin deeper: What does this tell you about Christ's centrality to all aspects of this universe?

Chapter 9: Jesus Shall Return

Jesus told his followers that he shall return to Earth to conclude the purpose of reality. After he returns, all humans, both the living and the dead, will become immortal, the Earth will be upgraded, and we will then be judged.

Christians have been waiting for Christ's return for thousands of years. Even today, millions are convinced that he will return very soon, perhaps within a few years.

The fact is that no one knows when Jesus will return. Jesus himself did not know. Apparently, he assumed it would occur during the lifetime of his first-century followers (Matt 24:34; Mark 13:30; Luke 21:32), but since the timing of his return was only known to the Father and Jesus explicitly stated that he does *not* know when he is supposed to return (Matt 24:35-39; Mark 13:31-37); the only thing a Christian can do is live their life in a manner where the Holy Spirit is constantly dwelling within them. And that occurs when we do our best to love God, our neighbor, and ourselves, and keep God's commandments.

9.1 Jesus Shall Return to Earth

Matthew 16:27 For the Son of Man will come in his Father's glory, and his angels shall accompany him. He will then judge all humans according to their works.

Matthew 25:31 When the Son of Man comes in his glory, accompanied by all the angels, he will sit on his glorious throne.

Mark 14:62 Jesus said, "I AM." He then added, "And you will see the Son of Man sitting on the right-hand side of Power, and coming on the clouds of heaven."

Matthew 24:30 And then the sign of the Son of Man will appear in heaven. And then all nations shall mourn and will see the Son of Man arrive on the clouds, with great power and glory.

Matthew 24:44 Therefore, be ready, for the Son of Man comes at a time you do not expect.

2 Thessalonians 1:7-10 To you who are being oppressed, rest assured that you will find relief together with us when the Lord Jesus appears from heaven with his mighty angels.

8 With a blast of flame, he will punish those who do not know God or refuse to obey the gospel of our Lord Jesus. 9 They will suffer eternal destruction, being expelled away from the Lord's presence and his glorious power, 10 when he comes to be glorified in his followers. Those who believe will be awestruck seeing him—including you because you believed our witness.

1 Thessalonians 3:13 *May he give you courage so that you will be found blameless and holy before God our Father when our Lord Jesus Christ comes with all his followers. Amen.*

1 Thessalonians 4:14-17 *For if we believe that Jesus died and rose again, we also believe that when Jesus returns, God will have those who have died having faith in Jesus accompany him.*

15 We tell you this directly from the Lord: His followers who will still be alive when the Lord comes will not precede those who have already died. 16 For the Lord himself will descend from heaven and will command, using the voice of an archangel and a blaring trumpet, for his dead followers to rise and meet him first. 17 After this happens, those of us who are still alive will rise into the air to meet the Lord among the clouds, and we will be with the Lord forever.

Hebrews 9:28 *So was Christ sacrificed just once to remove the sins of many. When he appears a second time, it will not be to deal with sin but to save those waiting for him.*

Acts 1:9-11 *After he had said these things, and while they were looking at him, he started floating up into the sky until he rose so high that a cloud hid him from their sight.*

10 As they looked intently toward the sky, two men in white robes suddenly appeared beside them. 11 They said, "Men of Galilee, why are you standing here staring into the sky? This same Jesus that you saw go up into the sky will return in the same manner he left."

1 Thessalonians 4:16 *For the Lord himself will descend from heaven and will command, using the voice of an archangel and a blaring trumpet, for his dead followers to rise and meet him first.*

Jesus Shall Return

Luke 12:40 You must be vigilant because the Son of Man will come when you do not expect him. (Also see Matt 24:36; Mark 13:32; 2 Pet 3:10)

Things to Ponder
1. Will Jesus return to Earth someday?
2. How will he return?

3. Who will accompany him?

4. What happens to the righteous Christian dead when Jesus is approaching Earth?

5. What happens to the righteous Christians who are still alive when Jesus is approaching Earth?

Jesus Shall Return | 227

6. *Can we anticipate when he will return, or will it be unexpected?*

7. *Think deeper: Why do you think it is vital for us not to know when Jesus will return? Explain.*

Chapter 10: Jesus Judges All

The Bible's closing imagery describes all humans who ever lived as standing before God to be judged. The identity of the one judging on behalf of God is also clearly identified: Jesus Christ, the "Son of Man."

10.1 Jesus Judges Humanity

Matthew 16:27 For the Son of Man will come in his Father's glory, and his angels shall accompany him. He will then judge all humans according to their works.

Matthew 25:31-34,41,46 When the Son of Man comes in his glory, accompanied by all the angels, he will sit on his glorious throne. 32 All of humanity will then stand before him, and he will separate them from one another just as a shepherd separates the sheep from the goats. 33 He will put the sheep on his right and the goats on his left. 34 Then the King will say to those assembled on his right, "Come, you whom my Father blesses, and inherit the kingdom that has been waiting for you since before the Earth's creation." . . . 41 Then he will say to those assembled on his left, "Leave my presence, you cursed! You are condemned to be cast into the eternal fire that was prepared for the devil and his followers." . . . 46 And they will leave and go into eternal punishment, while the righteous will go into eternal life.

John 5:22-30 *The Father does not judge anyone, but gave the authority to judge to the Son, 23 so that everyone may honor the Son just as they honor the Father. Whoever does not honor the Son is not honoring the one who sent him, the Father.*

24 I am telling you truthfully, those who listen to me and believe in him that sent me have eternal life. They will not be condemned—for they have crossed over from death to life.

25 I am telling you truthfully, the time has come and is now here when the dead shall hear the voice of the Son of God. Those who listen will live. 26 Just as the Father has life within himself, so has he also given the Son to have life within himself, 27 and gave him authority to judge because he is the Son of Man.

28 Do not be so surprised, because the time is coming when all those who are dead will hear his voice, 29 and will come out of the grave. Those who have lived righteously will receive a resurrection of life, while those who have been evil will receive a resurrection where they will be condemned.

30 I cannot do anything on my own but judge as I am instructed. My judgment is just because I am doing the will of the one who sent me and not my own will.

Revelation 20:10-15 *And the devil who deceived them was thrown into the lake of fetid fire, which also contained the beast and false prophet, and they will be tormented forever.*

11 And I saw a great white throne and the one who sat on it. The Earth and its sky vanished from his presence and could not be found anywhere. 12 I then saw the dead, both the powerful and the weak, standing before the throne. The books were opened, including the Book of Life, and the dead were judged according to their works, which were recorded in the books.

13 The sea gave up the dead who were in it, and Death and Hades gave up the dead that were in them—and each person was judged according to what they did. 14 Then Death and Hades were thrown into the lake of fire. The second death is the lake of fire. 15 Anyone whose name was not written in the Book of Life was cast into the lake of fire.

Revelation 22:12 *Look! I am coming quickly and will be bringing my reward to everyone based on what they have done.*

Acts 10:42 *Jesus commanded us to preach to the people and to witness that God ordained him to become the judge of the living and the dead.*

Acts 17:31 *God has set a date to righteously judge humankind by the man he has appointed. Proof that this is true is when he raised this man from the dead.*

2 Corinthians 5:10 *We must all stand before the judgment seat of Christ so that each of us will be judged based on what we have done in our lives, whether good or bad.*

2 Timothy 4:1 *I solemnly charge you before God and Christ Jesus, who will judge the living* *and the dead when he appears to establish his kingdom.*

1 Peter 4:5-6 *They will have to account for their actions to him, who is ready to judge the living and the dead.*

6 This is why the gospel is also preached to those who are now dead so that the same standard that judges the living will judge them, whereby they can also live with God in the spirit.

Things to Ponder
1. Who judges humanity? Why?

234 | This is Jesus Christ

> 2. Is there anyone who will not be judged?

> 3. What were the "books" that were opened that were used to evaluate the fate of everyone?

> 4. What is the fate of those whose names are not found in the "Book of Life"?

5. *What will happen to Satan and the truly evil like the Antichrist and false prophet?*

6. *Think deeper: Why is the Gospel also preached to those who are dead, such as those who have never had a chance while alive to accept him? What does this tell you about God's justice and mercy?*

Conclusion

You now possess the information you need to make an informed decision about how you can live your life. In addition, this book urges you to come to your own conclusions instead of relying upon the opinions of others. You are the master of your mind, and you decide what biblical passages mean to you.

Hopefully, you take the opportunity to write your thoughts in the Things to Ponder tables to ground your thoughts and give yourself a baseline to evaluate your beliefs as you grow.

Jesus Christ is not abstract – he is real, and his positive impact on your life is immense. You have natural rights, thanks to him. You have the comforts of the modern world, thanks to his influence. You owe it to yourself to understand who he is and whether you should align your life with his teachings.

At the end of the day, everything comes down to faith. But if you follow him and live as his disciple, you are *guaranteed* a life of meaning and joy no matter what evil happens to you.

I urge you to:

- Love God
- Love your neighbor
- Love yourself
- Keep God's commandments

Become the person that God wants you to be. Come unto Christ, follow him, live as his disciple, and endure to the end. Enjoy a life of meaning in this life and eternal joy in the next.

Scripture Reference Guide

Isaiah
Isa 53:6-11 6

Matthew
Matt 1:18-20 88
Matt 1:21 170
Matt 4:7 70
Matt 5:48 13
Matt 7:1-5 16
Matt 11:27 7
Matt 16:27 .... 222, 229
Matt 19:28 .... 45, 129
Matt 20:28 135
Matt 24:30 222
Matt 24:34 221
Matt 24:35-39 221
Matt 24:36 225
Matt 24:44 222
Matt 25:31 .... 45, 222
Matt 25:31-34,41,46 229
Matt 26:28 158
Matt 28:18 7
Matt 28:5-9 196
Matt 28:8-9 113

Mark
Mark 2:10 45
Mark 13:30 221
Mark 13:31-37 221
Mark 13:32 225
Mark 14:62 222
Mark 16:16 177

Luke
Luke 1:31-35 88
Luke 12:32 8
Luke 12:40 225
Luke 12:44 8
Luke 21:32 221
Luke 22:15-16,19-20 ... 158
Luke 22:29-30 .... 8, 45
Luke 22:42-44 158
Luke 22:69 45
Luke 24:36-46 113
Luke 24:36-51 197

John
John 1:1 .... 58, 71
John 1:1-3,10,14 .... 2, 53
John 1:3,10,14 .... 6, 122
John 1:12-13 7
John 1:14 .... 6, 92, 97
John 1:18 71
John 1:29 174
John 3:13-18 92
John 3:15-16,36 46
John 3:16 .... 6, 101
John 3:18 44

John 3:35 .... 7, 45
John 5:17-18,23 45
John 5:22-30 .... 46, 230
John 5:28-29 .... 45, 203
John 6:32-69 180
John 6:38-39 93
John 6:56 7
John 8:42 93
John 8:56-59 54
John 10:15 116
John 10:15,17-18 ..... 6, 144
John 10:17-18 196
John 10:30 .... 45, 80
John 10:38 79
John 13:3 7
John 13:31-32 79
John 14:6 .... 44, 217
John 14:7-12 44
John 14:10-11 45
John 14:10-11,20 80
John 14:20,23 7
John 15:1-11 7
John 15:7 26
John 15:10 45
John 16:15 8
John 16:28 44
John 17:5 .... 44, 84
John 17:5,22,24 62
John 17:10 8
John 17:11,21-23 ...... 7, 46, 80

John 17:19 .... 6, 139
John 17:22 .... 8, 46
John 20:28 71

Acts

Acts 1:1-11 198
Acts 1:9-11 224
Acts 4:10-12 217
Acts 10:40-41 199
Acts 10:42 232
Acts 10:43 177
Acts 13:37-39 177
Acts 17:31 232
Acts 20:28 71
Acts 20:32 7
Acts 26:18 7
Acts 26:23 6

Romans

Rom 1:3 .... 6, 101
Rom 3:23-25 139
Rom 5:2 8
Rom 5:6-8 .... 6, 145
Rom 5:9-11 150
Rom 5:10-11 187
Rom 5:19-21 165
Rom 6:9-10 .... 110, 200
Rom 6:10 117
Rom 8:3 .... 6, 98, 167
Rom 8:3,32 92
Rom 8:9-11 7
Rom 8:14-21 7

Rom 8:15,22-23 7
Rom 8:16-17 7
Rom 8:16-18 7
Rom 8:17 .... 7, 8
Rom 8:17-21,28-30 8
Rom 8:19-21 131
Rom 8:28-30 7
Rom 8:32 .... 8, 139
Rom 8:34 .... 110, 190
Rom 9:5 7
Rom 9:23-24 8
Rom 14:9 212

1 Corinthians
1 Cor 1:9 7
1 Cor 3:16-17 7
1 Cor 3:21-23 8
1 Cor 6:17 7
1 Cor 8:6 .... 6, 126
1 Cor 15:3 6
1 Cor 15:12-30 203
1 Cor 15:21 .... 6, 101
1 Cor 15:26 215
1 Cor 15:27 7
1 Cor 15:48-49 7

2 Corinthians
2 Cor 3:18 7
2 Cor 4:4 58
2 Cor 4:17 8
2 Cor 5:10 232
2 Cor 5:14-15 .... 6, 145

2 Cor 5:15 .... 110, 213
2 Cor 5:18-21 ...... 170, 187
2 Cor 5:19 80
2 Cor 5:21 97
2 Cor 6:10 8
2 Cor 8:9 .... 6, 7, 84

Galatians
Gal 1:4 .... 135, 170
Gal 2:20 7
Gal 2:20-21 .... 6, 145
Gal 3:13 135
Gal 3:26-29 7
Gal 3:26-4:7 7
Gal 3:29-4:7 7
Gal 4:4 .... 6, 92, 101

Ephesians
Eph 1:4 7
Eph 1:4-5 7
Eph 1:7 .... 159, 165
Eph 1:11-18 .... 7, 8
Eph 1:22 7
Eph 2:5-7 8
Eph 2:13-16 150
Eph 2:16 187
Eph 3:19 7
Eph 4:13,15,24 7

Philippians
Phil 2:5-7 58
Phil 2:5-8 .... 6, 84

Phil 2:6-8 63
Phil 2:7-8 .... 6, 101

Colossians

Col 1:12-13 7
Col 1:13-17 .... 6, 123
Col 1:15 59
Col 1:15-17 54
Col 1:16-20 8
Col 1:17 65
Col 1:19 .... 77, 88, 103
Col 1:20-22 .... 105, 150, 188
Col 1:27 .... 7, 8
Col 2:9 .... 77, 88, 103
Col 2:9-10 7
Col 3:4 8
Col 3:10 7
Col 3:24 7

1 Thessalonians

1 Thes 2:12 8
1 Thes 3:13 223
1 Thes 4:14-17 223
1 Thes 4:16 224
1 Thes 5:9-10 .... 6, 145

2 Thessalonians

2 Thes 1:7-10 222
2 Thes 1:12 71
2 Thes 2:13-14 8

1 Timothy

1 Tim 2:5 .... 191, 218
1 Tim 2:6 136

2 Timothy

2 Tim 1:9-10 54
2 Tim 1:10 .... 205, 215
2 Tim 2:10 8
2 Tim 2:12 8
2 Tim 4:1 232
2 Tim 4:7-8 8

Titus

Tit 2:13 71
Tit 2:14 .... 136, 171
Tit 3:7 7

Hebrews

Heb 1:2 7
Heb 1:2-3 .... 6, 58, 126
Heb 1:3 65
Heb 1:8-10 71
Heb 1:8-12 .... 6, 123
Heb 1:10-12 130
Heb 1:14 7
Heb 2:9 .... 6, 84
Heb 2:9-10 .... 6, 146
Heb 2:10 .... 6, 7, 8, 124
Heb 2:10-17 7
Heb 2:14-17 209
Heb 2:14-18 102
Heb 3:14 .... 7, 8

Heb 4:15 97
Heb 5:7-9 6
Heb 5:8 85
Heb 7:16 112
Heb 7:25 191
Heb 7:25-28 151
Heb 7:26 97
Heb 7:27 117
Heb 8:6 191
Heb 9:11-14 159
Heb 9:11-28 151
Heb 9:12,25-28 117
Heb 9:14 97
Heb 9:15 7
Heb 9:15,24 191
Heb 9:15,26-28 ....6, 146
Heb 9:26 162
Heb 9:28 224
Heb 10:10-14 118
Heb 10:10-20 139
Heb 12:9-10 7
Heb 12:24 191

James
Jas 1:12 8
Jas 2:5 ....7, 8

1 Peter
1 Pet 1:3-5 7
1 Pet 1:11 6
1 Pet 1:11,18-20 140
1 Pet 1:18-20 136

1 Pet 1:19-20 55
1 Pet 2:21-24 ....141, 171
1 Pet 2:22 97
1 Pet 2:24 167
1 Pet 3:18 .....118, 154, 167
1 Pet 4:5-6 233
1 Pet 5:4 8

2 Peter
2 Pet 1:1 72
2 Pet 1:3-4 ....7, 8
2 Pet 3:10 225
2 Pet 3:10-13 130

1 John
1 Jn 1:1-2 ....6, 55, 101
1 Jn 1:3-7 7
1 Jn 1:7 ....159, 174
1 Jn 2:1 192
1 Jn 2:1-2 171
1 Jn 2:13 55
1 Jn 2:29-3:3 7
1 Jn 3:2 205
1 Jn 3:5 97
1 Jn 3:5,8-9 174
1 Jn 3:9 7
1 Jn 4:2-3 ....6, 97
1 Jn 4:9-10 92
1 Jn 4:9-10,14 141
1 Jn 4:16-17 26
1 Jn 4:20-21 15
1 Jn 5:1-5 7

1 Jn 5:20 .... 7, 72

2 John

2 Jn 1:7 .... 6, 97

Revelation

Rev 1:5 .... 136, 154, 170, 172
Rev 1:6 8
Rev 1:18 ..... 112, 200, 205, 210
Rev 3:14 .... 6, 126
Rev 3:21 8
Rev 5:5,9,12 108
Rev 5:9 154
Rev 5:10 8
Rev 7:17 218
Rev 20:10-15 231
Rev 20:11 131
Rev 20:13-14 215
Rev 20:4 8
Rev 21:1,5 130
Rev 21:7 7
Rev 22:12 232
Rev 22:5 8

Index

Abide in Christ 26
Abyss, The 23, 43
Act. Do not be content to be acted upon...........51
Anglican/Independent Catholic.....................26
Atheism.....................5, 22
Behavior, not interpretation is important.......9, 21, 40, 178
Biblical writers were not being ironic 3
Bride of Christ
   Need to be within her body to be saved.....21
C.S. Lewis 46
Charity
   The greatest attribute..........14, 15, 165
Children of God, The 7
   Adopted by the Father 5, 7, 11, 15
   Become God's heirs 7, 10, 12
   Shall rule over the universe as Christ's fellow-heirs.... 7, 8, 11
   Share in God's divine nature.......... 7, 11, 14
   Share in God's glory ... 8
   Share in God's oneness and mutual indwelling......... 7, 11
Christian God
   Altruistic deity.......... 10
   Motivations of........... 11
Christian living 21
Christian milieu 29, 32
Christian morality....... 20
   Created an artificial floor that lifted humanity above its core nature 24
   Made our lives better 24
Christian worship services..................... 19
Christianity
   World's largest religion.................. 29

Church
Importance of membership in a ... 21, 26
Churches
Change if you are unhappy 26
Civilizational collapse 23, 24
Compatibility with God
God's desire for us 11, 12, 14, 26
Conservatism 39
Consumerism 21
Continually repent 16
Cosmology 121, 122
Creator of the universe
Jesus Christ 3, 6, 8, 121, 122, 125, 127
Creator, The
Became human 6
Motivations and actions 8
Eastern Christian 26
Empathetic morality ... 32
Eternal life, Obtain 3, 238
Eternal principles 43
Face value of text 2, 3
False gods 10
Fog of temptation 9
Founding Fathers 33
Galaxies, Trillions of 6, 121
God
Is rational 12
Motivations of 8, 11
Perfection of 13
God is real
Knowledge that 40
God of love 11, 13, 14, 26, 52
God wants us to be happy 10, 11
God's Commandments
Are designed to make us people who love 13, 14
God's glory
Humans are 11
God's love 40
Golden Rule 36, 39
Good people can disagree 25
Guardrails prevent us from accidentally falling off 9, 12, 16
Have a family 4
Hedonism 5, 22
Holy Spirit, The
Witnesses of the Son of God 40

Index

Homo sapiens sapiens 53, 101
Human brain, The
   A very powerful computer 1
Human equality 32
Human mortality 3
Human nature values insiders over outsiders 22, 23, 33, 43
Humans
   Want to be "good" and do good 9
Humans share the same urges and motivations 10
Inability to tell right from wrong 43
Innate human dignity 32
Intellectual honesty 2, 3, 52
Interpretation is subjective 25
Interpretation of biblical passages 1, 2, 3, 51
Jesus Christ
   Became human 97
   Came from the Father 44
   Equal to the Father 45
   Follow 40
   Forgives sins 45
   God made flesh 44
   His followers receive eternal life 46
   Importance of 1
   Influence of 17, 29
   Is God 46, 53
   Is my God 47
   Judges all 46, 229
   Makes all humans immortal 195
   Moral teaching of 17
   Much more than a prophet or teacher 46
   Mutually indwells with the Father 45
   Neccessity of 20
   One with the Father .. 45
   Only way to the Father 44
   Our Savior 26, 135
   Receives the universe for an inheritance 45
   Requires us to obey him 45
   Resurrection of 195
   Return to 43

Returned to the Father 44
Saves us from death ... 45
Shares glory 11, 46
Shares oneness and mutual indwelling 11, 14, 46
Shares rule over the universe 13, 45
Sits on the Father's right-hand side 45
Son of the Father 3
The Father's only Son 44
The only way 217
The Son of God 87
Upgrades Earth 45, 129
We see the Father when looking at him 44
Will "marry" his Bride (the Church) at the Last Day 21
Will return 45

Jesus Christ, Moral teachings
  The weakest outsider has equal worth to the most powerful insider 23

Jesus is Lord 25
Jesus, Return of 221
Jesus, taught how to live 42
Join forces to save our civilization 23, 24, 25, 39
Judge without hypocrisy 16
Judgment Day 1
Keep God's commandments 4, 12, 13, 14, 15, 16, 25, 45, 221, 238
Keep God's commandments 43
Legacy
  Desire to leave a 3
Life trajectory 2
Living as Christ's disciple guarantees a life of meaning and joy 9, 237
Love God 4, 14, 42, 238
Love your neighbor 4, 14, 43, 238
Love yourself 4, 15, 43, 238
Meaningful life 3, 10, 15, 25, 42, 52, 238

Modern STEM world 17, 25, 29, 35
Moral right 1, 29, 30
Narcissism 5
Natural rights 22, 29, 30, 35
   Are not self-evident in nature 33
   Are reciprocal 30
   Float on air 31
   Founded on Christ's moral teachings 22, 29, 39
   Freedom of mind 1, 51
   Make the weakest outsider equal to the most powerful insider 30
   Your most important rights 17, 18, 22, 23, 25, 26, 29, 30, 31, 32, 33, 34, 35, 38, 39, 237
Nihilism 5
Obey God 12
Ockham's logic 41
Our choice has eternal consequences 12
Path that leads to eternal life 4, 5, 8, 9, 10, 12, 15, 16, 44

Progeny, Desire for
   God's motivation 11
Protestant 26
Roman Catholic 25
Science 41, 121
Slavery 22, 24, 33, 35, 36, 102, 210
Spirituality without religion 21
Subjective communication from God 40
Testable evidence for God 22
The Church is the Bride of Christ 21
The Church of Jesus Christ of Latter-day Saints 25
This book does not tell you what to believe 1, 51, 237
Track record of living Christ's moral teachings 17
True happiness comes from becoming compatible with the God of love 11, 26, 52

Two-tiered justice system 23
Tyranny 23
Universal debt to Jesus because of his followers 35, 36, 44, 237
Universe .. 2, 5, 6, 7, 8, 11, 13, 15, 16, 46, 60, 66, 67, 121, 122, 132, 221
Usurp God's judgment authority over you
Uncharitable dogmatists *1*
Value of humans within the Christian worldview is incalculable 6, 9
We are commanded to become perfect 13
We are free to obey or disobey God 12
We change as we mature 1, 52, 237
Western churches lost their zeal and grew silent 19
Western civilization 29
Greatest civilization in history *17, 18*

Moral foundation *24, 26, 29, 37, 38, 39, 40*
Moral foundation is being destroyed *38, 39*
Wisdom comes with maturity 10
Word became human, The 3
Word of God, The
A guardrail to hold on to *9*
Word was God, The 2
World, Trillions of 6, 121
Worldview 5, 8, 9, 10, 17, 53
You are free to believe whatever you want 1, 51, 237
You are more valuable than any world or galaxy 6, 11
You can share everything Christ has 6
You do not need anyone to tell you what to believe 1, 51
You exist 5

ABOUT THE AUTHOR

Edward K. Watson has over 70,000 hours in writing, editing, and analyzing complex documents such as RFPs, proposals, and project execution plans for very large projects, including a dozen in the billion-dollar range. He is the author of the four-volume *Is Jesus "God"? A Witness to the World That Jesus is the Christ, the Eternal God*. The work details the only empirical evidence that anyone can use to justify the belief that the Holy Bible is inspired by God (*the New Testament is a frameless, unharmonized, correlative anthology*). The book also provides three additional pieces of evidence that support belief in God and demolishes atheism.

He published his first book in 1998 (**Mormonism**), but lost interest in Latter-day Saint apologetics and discontinued the series. After a decade as an atheist, he is, once again, a devout member of The Church of Jesus Christ of Latter-day Saints and has enormous appreciation for the teachings in the Holy Bible and Book of Mormon concerning our God, Jesus Christ, and of his infinite Atonement.

Ed defends Christianity as a whole and supports the faith of all Christians regardless of their church. He prefers to build bridges rather than destroy homes. He found Jesus in his church and recognizes others find Him in different churches. Ed does not concern himself with arguments concerning biblical interpretation since he recognizes that those who insist others must believe their interpretation of specific text to be

252 | This is Jesus Christ

saved usurp Christ's judgment authority over us. *If God never said we must interpret a passage in a specific way to be saved, then no one else can either.* Christ, alone, decides our eternal fate. Those who condemn others to eternal torture in hell for not believing the same thing they do will be accountable for their uncharitable actions. He takes Christ's words seriously:

> *You will be judged with the same standard that you judge others; you will be measured with the same measure you use on others. (Matthew 7:2)*

It only took thirty years, thousands of books, and tens of thousands of dollars, but Ed is finally starting to understand that what is truly important in life is not what he knows, but who he is as a person. He finally gets what the Savior said when he told us to:

- LOVE GOD
- LOVE YOUR NEIGHBOR
- LOVE YOURSELF
- KEEP THE COMMANDMENTS

To be truly wise and content means to live a life of meaning, where we genuinely love. We can then leave this world with joy, knowing that as God is, so are we (1 John 4:16-17).

www.ingramcontent.com/pod-product-compliance
Lightning Source LLC
Chambersburg PA
CBHW072224200426
43209CB00073B/1931/J